ZEN
GARDENS

ZEN GARDENS

ERIK BORJA

PHOTOGRAPHS BY PAUL MAURER

WARD LOCK

*To the memory of Frédéric Ditis, whose
wisdom, humanity and understanding
accompanied me throughout my researches.
He was, and will always be, my exemplar and
my teacher.*

CONTENTS

'Now what is called "art", because it appeases the minds of all people and arouses emotion in the great and humble alike, could be the starting point of increased longevity and happiness, a way of prolonging life.'

Zeami Motokiyo (1363–1443),
'The Secret Tradition of the Nogaku' (1418),
in *The Sakuteiki*

INTRODUCTION

To say that the urge to create has its source in infancy is considered something of a cliché, but as I approach my fiftieth birthday I am forced to wonder about the strange pilgrimage that led me from Algiers, where I was born, the epitome of a Mediterranean town, to the gardens of Kyoto, Japan's symbolic places.

As a child I was delicate and a rather introverted dreamer, and I kept aloof from games with other children of my own age and spent my time with modelling clay, building secret little worlds into which I escaped. At this time my family lived in an apartment with a terraced extension, on which my mother grew pot plants. One day someone gave us one of those little 'Japanese gardens' that florists were making at the time. Landscaped miniature plants, among which little ornaments, such as a pagoda and a bridge, had been placed, were arranged in a ceramic pot, creating a childlike, fairytale image of Japan. I was fascinated by the arrangement, although I can no longer remember the details, and it encouraged my daydreams and my passion for creativity. The small scale, the limited space, the arrangement, the artifice and subject matter seduced me. This microcosm

overwhelmed the natural magnificence of the plants my mother grew, reducing them to the status of objects. 'Transcendence of reality' was the principle that I felt but did not understand, and it was a principle that would influence my life and lead me in unforeseeable creative directions.

I did not shine academically, and only history, geography and drawing interested me. My father therefore decided to enrol me at the École des Beaux Arts when I was fifteen years old, and of all the subjects taught there, I liked sculpture and modelling best. The sensual pleasure I felt when I touched the clay, the physical action of cutting it, the fascination of the play of light and shade, rather than the line or flat tint, all contributed to guiding my creativity towards the three-dimensional and to making it my favourite subject.

Having become a sculptor, I strove in all my works to suggest rather than to make manifest what it was that fed my imagination. My inspiration drew, of course, on reality, but it was the emotions that reality inspired in me that I tried to convey – the representation of the poetic sensibility aroused by an object seemed more interesting than the object itself.

In 1963 I went to Paris to study, and my first exhibition was held in 1966 at the gallery of Iris Cler, who became my dealer. There was, however, always something missing in this wonderful city, and my need for nature could never be satisfied by the parks that are provided for this purpose. They are too urban and dominated by buildings – as in the Tuileries Gardens or Luxembourg Gardens – or too visibly man-made – as in the parks around the Boulevard Haussmann. Only the alpine garden in the Botanical Gardens provided an acceptable, if 'civilized', view of nature. In this restricted, enclosed space I spent long hours travelling in my mind, forgetting the city around me.

It was at the beginning of the 1970s when I was staying in the Drôme area where my family had settled that I discovered the family property. It was a small house in ruins, wedged between the vines and a hill, at the foot of which flowed a river. I immediately liked the place. It had been abandoned long ago, and there was no garden, only a sorry-looking field overrun with brambles, but I decided to make it my refuge, somewhere I could come from time to time to recharge my energies. Once the building had been restored, I turned my attention to the garden.

I could not have guessed that the planting of the first tree, an apparently insignificant act, would alter the course of my life. I had no technical knowledge and no substantial funds, but after a good deal of trial and error, I produced the preliminary version of a garden on which I am still working today, twenty-five years later.

The interest I had had in Japanese gardens since my youth had led me to collect numerous books over the years, and in the spring of 1977 I had an opportunity to visit Japan. I landed in Kyoto late one night and was staying in a run-of-the-mill international hotel. Too excited to sleep, I went out into the street. I quickly left the main road and made my way through an alley lined with traditional houses. Maidenhair trees (*Ginkgo biloba*), clipped like large bonsai trees, lined the pavements. Beyond them, tiny gardens, clearly designed by the residents, provided passers-by with a wide variety of miniature landscapes.

Then, in front of the entrance to a garage, between two petrol pumps and level with the pavement, I noticed a rectangle of unfired bricks containing an arrangement of five stones on a bed of white gravel. There were no plants, just a little moss. I experienced an inexplicable emotion, almost a sense of shock, similar to the feeling that has sometimes swept through me as I stood before some Western works of art. But the sensation that overwhelmed me here had nothing in common with the emotions aroused by a sculpture by Michelangelo or a painting by Picasso. There were just five stones, the largest of which measured barely 30 centimetres (12 inches), and some gravel, all crowded between two petrol pumps!

It was as if I had found the key, as if I had finally been given the code that would enable me to understand a work of art that would reveal not only beauty but also the way to achieve harmony between the world and myself.

The remainder of my stay in Japan and my studies of the numerous gardens I visited there reinforced the feeling that I had found a form of creativity in which the little boy I had been, making a world of his own, could come alive again and find expression. The rest is a logical sequel to this episode. I left Paris in 1979 and moved my studio to the Drôme, with the intention of devoting one or two hours a day to my garden. But this arrangement quickly changed, and the garden became my studio.

Since then I have continued my researches into those always-changing places and into the places I have had the good fortune to design for garden lovers who are as passionate about these gardens and fascinated by them as I am.

Factors Influencing a Garden

Man and the Environment

Humans observed and experienced nature for millions of years before they were able to begin to draw lessons from it and use it to emerge from their subhuman condition. From the dawn of history, geography and climate have had an effect on our evolution and have influenced our behaviour. Almost everything that contributes to human society depends on the natural environment in which that society has been created and has developed. The character of individual peoples and their religion and politics, as well as their habitat, clothing, food and customs, bear the imprint of their environment.

Nature

All the peoples of the world have been created both in harmony with nature and in opposition to it. Often generous, sometimes capricious, nature may take back in an instant what it has provided for long periods, and it is likely that from this atavistic relationship of acceptance and fear are born those primary mythologies and religions in which nature in its various forms is perceived as emanating from the divine.

Paradise Gardens

The jigsaw that is the peoples of the earth provides numerous interpretations of this relationship between nature and the divine, but a constant thread can be found running through the myths. This is the idea of a paradise, a word that derives from the Persian word *paridaiza*, meaning garden. Paradise, which is a reward for those who have been able to leave behind their primitive natures and elevate their souls, is the kingdom of harmony, where humans, released from their earthly constraints, live in harmony with the divine, with the whole.

Images of paradise differ from religion to religion, but idealized nature is a constant feature, acting as a framework for, and background to, this meeting between humankind and the divine.

This ever-present idea of the paradise garden in the history of humanity can also be understood as a manifestation of nostalgia for early innocence – before the Fall – and, more prosaically, for childhood.

In the West, after Judeo-Christian thinking had supplanted the old beliefs, humans found themselves at the centre of the world, chosen by God to have dominion over and to subdue untamed nature for their own benefit. The ensuing image of paradise, marked by humankind's predominance, has certain similarities to a structured, organized garden, in which tamed and ordered nature offers delights only to those souls who have been chosen to enjoy eternity.

In the East the place taken by humans in the universe is perceived differently. People are part of a whole, in the same way as are all the elements

Above:

The Amitabha paradise depicted in a Taima mandala. During the Heian period (794–1185) many temples and monasteries were inspired by the Chinese view of paradise represented by a *shinden*-style house.

Right:

An eighteenth-century Indian miniature. In the West and parts of the East a highly structured view of the garden asserted itself, which was very different from the naturalistic view that endures in the rest of the East, particularly in Japan.

that make up the world, and they share with those elements a fragment of divinity. This sense of uniqueness and of universality is found in all the philosophical and religious movements that have crossed Asia from India to Japan and that have developed a relationship with nature. The Eastern paradise is informed more by untamed and striking, real or mythical landscapes, and by areas inhabited by the gods.

Shintoism and Buddhism

At the beginning of our period, when the remarkable civilizations in China and Korea were reaching their peak, Japan was isolated from the mainland by a hostile sea and inhabited by an almost primitive society, which lived by fishing and hunting and by growing rice. This population, born of successive waves of immigration, regarded itself as the hosts of a land that belonged to the gods and to the spirits of the ancestors, whom they revered. Arising from geographical, climatic and cultural circumstances that differed from those found in the neighbouring continent, their first religion, Shintoism, celebrated a divided nature. The unstable nature of the islands, where earthquakes and typhoons are frequent occurrences, was made up for by the favourable climate resulting from the monsoon and by rice cultivation, on which Japanese civilization is based. Wild and turbulent, but also generous, this nature is both feared and revered in its various manifestations. It was probably this dual perception of nature that influenced the

Opposite:

A Shinto shrine on the slopes of Mount Kujo, Kyoto, celebrating a sacred spring where the *kami* (spirits) live.

A Heian shrine in Kyoto, dating from the Meiji period (1868–1912). Built in 1894 to commemorate the 1100th anniversary of Kyoto, which is otherwise known as Heian-Kyo, it is a magnificent example of the *shinden* style.

Opposite:

Sacred rope hangs at the entrance to a Shinto shrine in Kyoto.

emergence of a cult around it. The inhabitants of the archipelago formulated the Shinto religion as a code of good conduct between humans and nature. Shrines were built on mountains and in clearings. Certain trees, rocks or waterfalls, regarded as the home of the spirits, the *kami*, became the objects of a cult. Such places, which were famed for the sacred essence emanating from them, became revered and are still the site of pilgrimages. They were meeting points between mankind and the divine.

From the sixth century onwards peaceful contacts took place between the mainland and the archipelago, and Japan was able to assimilate Sino-Korean culture, which became the motive force behind fundamental changes. Chinese writing was adopted, and sciences, the arts and philosophical and religious trends were favourably received and integrated into the existing concept of thought.

The innovations ushered in a period of reorganization and structuring of Japanese society, which had previously been fluid. During the Heian period (794–1185) Buddhism spread within Japanese aristocracy and gradually permeated all levels of society. Numerous temples and monasteries were built on the continental model around the imperial court in Nara and, later, in Kyoto. Without entirely abandoning Shintoism, the Japanese adopted doctrines imported from China by Buddhist monks.

Chinese paintings represent paradise as a house, known as a *shinden*, accompanied by five pavilions, one to the north and four on the sides facing the northwest, northeast, southwest and southeast. They were linked by raised, covered passages and surrounded by gardens. In front of the *shinden* was a pool, in the centre of which was an island in the form of a mountain, connected with the shore by an arched bridge (*soriba-shi*). The basic elements of the garden – the lake, the island and the mountain – which appear in this scheme will recur in various forms throughout our study. From the seventh century the Japanese aristocracy adopted this Chinese model of the celestial home of the Buddha, the Paradise of the Pure Land, for its own houses. Gradually, however, the gardens, which had adorned them until the twelfth century, and the idea of paradise associated with them developed from the initial scheme, and as it came into contact with Confucianism and Taoism Buddhism gave rise to several trends and different interpretations of paradise. The Taoist tradition, for example, imagined paradise as a group of island mountains floating on the ocean, inaccessible to humans and peopled with immortal beings. Supported on the back of turtles, the islands drifted over eastern seas.

When the Japanese discovered this myth, they were certain that Japan was this archipelago of the blessed and that their early religion, Shintoism, meant that their islands were the home of the

Left:

The fourteenth-century garden of Tenryu-ji, Kyoto, which dates from the Kamakura period (1185–1333). It was designed by Muso Kokushi for the shogun Ashigaka Takanji. Inspired by Chinese paintings of the Sung period, this garden breaks with the *shinden* style of the Heian period and may be regarded as the first garden to have a specifically Japanese character.

gods. Natural sites influenced these evocations of paradise, and the Japanese landscape as a whole gradually replaced the Chinese model, which was bound by stereotypes associated with the layout of the celestial home.

Although the architecture of temples and houses continued to use the Chinese model (*shinden*) until the twelfth century, the surrounding gardens differed somewhat. Japanese sensibilities are inconsistent with the rather formal organization of the Chinese model, and garden makers relaxed the *shinden* scheme considerably because it was too rigid, moving towards a more sensitive, less precise elegance that was closer not only to the characteristics of their land but also to their ancestral belief in the special relationship they maintained with their landscape through Shintoism. These juxtapositions of influences gave a style of garden that used all the resources provided by nature for gardeners. In accordance with Buddhist teaching, these gardens reflected the rhythm of the seasons, the feeling of transience and the cosmic order. The result was similar to a landscape art that can be described as naturalistic, even if strong symbolism and strict guidelines governed their design.

Because the development of religious thought and of the style of gardens are inseparable, it is likely that garden design encouraged thought and helped move it in new directions, towards the Zen approach. This Japanese style became more widespread from the end of the twelfth century onwards.

The doctrine, which had originated in China and was a branch of Buddhism, was studied and then imported into Japan by monks. Rather than being thought of as a religion or philosophy, it

Above:

The Golden Pavilion in the garden of Rokuon-ji, Kinkaku-ji, Kyoto, dates from the fourteenth century and was designed in the Kamakura period (1185–1333). The vast pool, which is dotted with numerous islands planted exclusively with pines, lies to the south of the pavilion that is reflected in it.

Pages 20–21:

The garden of the Tenryu-ji, Kyoto. The rocky promontory (*deshina*), positioned in front of the main building (*hojo*), is surrounded by low planting so that the general view of the garden is not obscured.

may be regarded as a way of life through which thought and action could combine to enable people to free themselves from socio-cultural conventions and become ready to find their inner selves, their Buddhist nature. Arising from a philosophy that upset traditions in China from the sixth century on, Zen assumed an even more radical form in Japan. It rejected the customary religious representations, changed liturgies, gave priority to the garden over the pagoda, went some way towards secularizing the relationships between humans and the divine and individualized this process. The gardens went along with this development in religious thought and, in diverging from the models of the Heian period, achieved a more refined and timeless, almost abstract, representation of nature.

The Zen Approach

Inspired by the Shinto tradition and enriched by Chinese and Korean culture, the garden acquired its specifically Japanese character through the application of the Zen philosophy.

The Tenryu-ji garden in Kyoto marked this transition from the *shinden* style to the Zen style. Laid out on the site of an ancient imperial residence and converted by the monk Muso Kokushi into a Zen monastery in 1342, the garden underwent profound changes. It had originally been designed as a pleasure garden and consisted of an extensive pool on which small boats sailed and which was dotted with islands large enough to accommodate a small orchestra. Muso Kokushi reduced the scale considerably by adjusting the design to change it into a meditation garden, which was visible in its entirety from the main room of the monastery. Arrangements of stones were added to the focal points of the composition, among which was a dry fall, one of the first examples of the metaphoric use of water. A hill in the distance provided a backdrop for the pool, and during the Heian period, in a continuation of the Buddhist tradition, the garden was integrated into the wider landscape, where the plants marked the passing of the seasons

The refined style continued to be used throughout the *shoin* period during the thirteenth and fourteenth centuries. The term *shoin* describes the typically Japanese style of architecture that replaced the originally Chinese *shinden* style.

In a move away from symmetry, houses and monasteries began to be built in complex, irregular designs, which made careful use of limited spaces, often enclosed by walls, for increasingly small gardens. The suggested landscapes often tended towards abstraction.

What the newcomer to the style notices first about a Zen garden is the change in scale compared with the natural order of things. In the same way as in paintings, when a landscape is portrayed on the two-dimensional and limited surface of the canvas or paper, this type of garden, enclosed as it is in a confined space, has more similarities with the graphic arts of the Sung dynasty in China (960–1279) than with the paradise gardens of earlier times. Designed to be gazed at from a fixed point – that is, from the raised, covered passage of the house – it is seen in its entirety and so transforms the way we see it.

The Ryoan-ji garden in Kyoto, which is attributed to Soami (late fifteenth to early sixteenth century) is the most eloquent example of this. Fifteen stones, arranged in five groups of two, three and five, are spread out in front of the wall of the building over a flat, sandy, rectangular area of 200 square metres (2150 square feet), which is bordered on the south and west by a low cob wall. The space occupied by the stones is tiny compared with the gravel surface, but there is the impression of vastness, despite the modest size of the rocky outcrops. This use of emptiness with *niwa* – that is, a gravel surface surrounding a Shinto shrine or the space set aside for ritual ceremonies in front of the temple walls – emphasizes the subjective power of the stone composition, which brings it to life and highlights the stone relief.

The virtual absence of vegetation (there is only a little moss on the stones) contributes to the illusion

of an immense landscape, suggesting a distant view of a group of islands on the ocean. The complete absence of detail, the lack of ornamentation and the restraint in the stones chosen combined with their rhythm on the luminous, uniform surface of the gravel help to train the observers, who may, by escaping from the reality that engulfs them, reach a state of awareness through meditation.

It is the imposition of absolute asymmetry that makes the Ryoan-ji garden a shining example of the control of space, where emptiness and shape are interchangeable as they together contribute to the magnificent balance.

Recalling mythical or real landscapes and metaphorically representing the universe, these three-dimensional pictures are to some extent the physical props or tools encouraging us to look for our original nature. Free from any dogma, they meet a need for harmony and communion with the universe as a whole.

'Emptiness reveals fullness, as sound gives shape to silence, Indian ink to white paper.'

The garden of Tenryu-ji, Kyoto. At the entrance to the site is a representation of Mount Shumisen (Sumeru in Chinese), the centre of the Buddhist universe. It was constructed in 1987 by Saburo Sone.

The garden of Ryogen-in, Daitoku-ji, Kyoto. This contemporary interpretation of the *karesansui* (dry garden) is distinguished by the choice of imposing stones, which are enhanced by the way the gravel is raked. The gravel plays an important part in this composition.

Above:

The garden of Ryogen-in, Daitoku-ji, Kyoto, is attributed to Soami (*c*.1500). It is a classical composition of an erect stone, accompanied by horizontal and low-lying stones. The slight incline of the tall stone gives a particular dynamic to this evocation of Mount Shumisen.

Right:

A detail of the eastern portion of the garden of Daisen-in, Daitoku-ji, Kyoto. The profusion of stones, their quality and appearance are in keeping with the narrow space, which forms a corner with the building. They form a varied landscape, which expands like a folding screen but can never be viewed in its entirety. The inspiration of wash drawings of the Sung period is evident here.

Dominated as it was by the Zen theme, the *shoin* period imposed its identity on garden design and gave it its originality and typically Japanese character. From the seventeenth century there was a return to a less austere, more playful and more picturesque style, which distanced itself somewhat from the rigour and severity of the previous period and which extended at the same time into imperial and aristocratic residences. The accumulation of themes in these gardens, which were again designed for walking in, makes them richer and more varied and at the same time less metaphysical and more recreational.

Nevertheless, the Zen style continued to be used in the temples, and the ethos and approach lived on in innumerable variations, which serve to illustrate and illuminate the history of the gardens of Japan from the thirteenth century until the present.

Right:

The garden of Shoden-ji, Kyoto, which is attributed to Mirei Shigemori (*c*.1600), consists entirely of azaleas in three groups of three, five and seven (*sichigosan*). In clear weather the arrangement frames an interesting view of Mount Hiei, which dominates Kyoto.

Below:

The garden of the *hojo* (the main building of the monastery) at Nanzen-ji, Kyoto. Designed in the seventeenth century, this triangular arrangement of stones, which decrease in height from left to right, is accompanied by plants, the size of which keeps the overall scale small.

Pages 32–3:

The garden of Taizo-in, Myoshin-ji, Kyoto, was completed by the architect Nakane Kinsaku in the 1960s. The interpretation is faithful to Zen philosophy in spirit – it is a garden for contemplation, not for walking in – but it differs in shape, for the entire garden is designed around an actual large stream, rather than the metaphorical representation of a stream.

The orchards seen from the tea garden in the gardens designed by Erik Borja in the Drôme. The lonicera bushes in the foreground have been clipped into the shape of hills.

REVEALING THE ESSENCE OF NATURE

'Life begins on the day you start a garden.'
Chinese proverb

There are many books available today that provide accurate information about the art of the gardens of Japan, but, as with all art forms, photographic reproductions and written descriptions are no substitute for actually seeing the objects. What we look for in art is, above all, emotion, which is something that cannot touch us or affect us at second-hand, just as studying the mechanics of a work of literature does not necessarily reveal the essence of the poetry.

A single visit to one of the gardens in Kyoto is worth all the books written on the subject. Sadly, however, Japan is far away, and few people have the opportunity to visit it. Nevertheless, the lessons we can draw from reading about the gardens there can help to make us aware of nature and teach us to look at it in a different way and to gain a better understanding of certain styles of expression, which we can then introduce into our own gardens, according to our individual preferences and personal taste.

Let us not forget that apart from magnificent landscape design, the garden in Japan is primarily intended to provide us with a space where, through activity and meditation, we can reach a state of awareness that is in harmony with the forces of nature. On a more modest note, it is important to emphasize the activity – that is, the physical effort involved in making and maintaining a garden. This process is one of enlightenment. It reveals inner resources of which we have previously been unaware, and it transforms our body, feeds our mind and contributes to a new awareness of ourselves. It teaches us patience and humility, as well as tenacity, but above all it forces us to be as one with nature so that we may understand it better and, though our communion with it, be able to reveal its essence.

I hope that, through this description of my own path, you will be encouraged to embark on the adventure of making a garden, which may be both a place of experience and activity as well as space for serenity and happiness.

Opposite:

In Erik Borja's garden in the Drôme the tightly clipped plants highlight the emerging rocks and act as a foreground to the vast landscape beyond, which is thereby incorporated into the garden.

Above:

A view of Erik Borja's garden in the Drôme from the south of the pools.

Choosing the Site

In Japan, throughout the *shinden* era (794–1185), houses and gardens were built according to the principles of Chinese cosmogony. From their inception, they provided the best orientations, protecting them from harmful influences. The garden here protects the house. In China, when the emperor moved around, his temporary residences were surrounded by temporary gardens, in which the role of the rocks, arranged and positioned according to their colour or shape, was to correct the imperfections of the site and protect it from the evil spirits outside. All these rules, which were gathered together at the end of the twelfth century by the monk Yoshitsune Gokyohoko in *The Sakuteiki*, a treatise on Japanese gardens, may seem esoteric to us, but if we look at them more closely

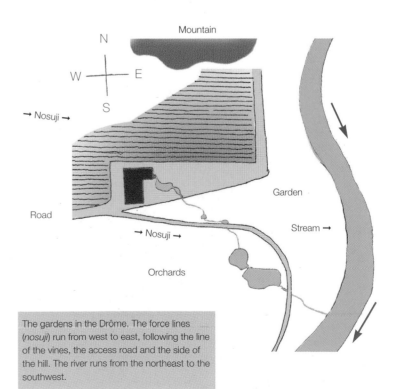

The gardens in the Drôme. The force lines (*nosuji*) run from west to east, following the line of the vines, the access road and the side of the hill. The river runs from the northeast to the southwest.

Left:

In the garden of Ryoan-ji, Kyoto, the main island is reflected in the large pool below the dry garden. The large plants in the foreground are in harmony with the scale of the site and the mountain that dominates it.

Right:

A hanging garden in Paris, which was designed by Erik Borja in 1993, where the rocky outcrops are designed to counterbalance the towers of La Défense in the distance.

we can discern the logic, which arises from an awareness of natural phenomena and of the resulting influences, good or bad, on humans.

It is appropriate to take the rules into account and if, as is often the case, the chosen site does not meet the criteria recommended as ideal, the gardener who is laying out the garden will have to change the topography of places through the use of clever devices to make them conform to the required orientations.

This is the approach I have instinctively followed in developing my own garden. For several years in succession, whenever I visited my family, my footsteps always led me to the same place: to the ruined house on the slope, which dominated the landscape and the river flowing below. The attraction was so strong that I decided to camp there to feel the good 'vibrations'. They seemed to be so good that the restoration of the house started the following year. When the work was complete, I planned the broad lines of my future garden. Its development improved the site considerably, eliminating its imperfections, gradually making it merge with its surroundings, enhancing the harmonious atmosphere and, in so doing, heightening the sense of well-being I felt when I stayed there.

Later, when I read the texts in *The Sakuteiki*, I noticed that the orientations and geographical situation of my garden were generally close to the ideal model and that my work on the land had merely reinforced its qualities.

Left:

The garden of Tenryu-ji, Kyoto, was one of the earliest examples of a garden in which the *shinden* style was abandoned for an entirely Japanese theme. Some of the features introduced into this garden heralded the development of the Zen garden.

Tayori, Fusui and Nosuji

After choosing the site but before designing the garden, it is vital to absorb the spirit of the place, to study its geographical and climatic characteristics and to observe the way light falls throughout the year. This knowledge helps us to understand the garden's subjective and objective structure, its *tayori*, and enables us to express its poetic emotion or *fusui*. The lines of force of the chosen landscape, the *nosuji* (nerve, tendon), along which energies flow, must also be taken into account. They will determine the main outlines of the garden's structure and make it possible to incorporate the garden into the overall site.

All these details are part of the thinking that must take place before a garden is created and that will help it to succeed.

This approach is easier to follow when a place is already familiar to us, but it should always be an essential part of the process. When we want to create a garden, we must have plenty of time at our disposal, because when we are faced with a blank sheet and have a project in mind, impatience makes us want to proceed too quickly. A period of thoughtfulness, of reflection and of stillness will, paradoxically, give us more time because we will avoid making errors.

The preparatory period should be taken up with making rough outline sketches and drawings of the proposed garden, as I do when I am working to a client's brief and have to explain my plans with sketches. These drawings are not an exact representation of what will be created, but they do give an idea of the atmosphere I want to achieve and the overall way in which the space will be organized in its wider environment.

Even though I produce drawings, I still like to mark out the space on the ground by using a stick to show the outlines of such features as the pool, the direction of the water and where soil will be removed, and to indicate the height of hills and rocky outcrops, and the site of clumps of plants and trees with bamboo canes. By indicating the positions of the main features in this way, it is possible to modify, refine and finalize my intentions in the actual space in which the garden will be created and to prepare for the next stage.

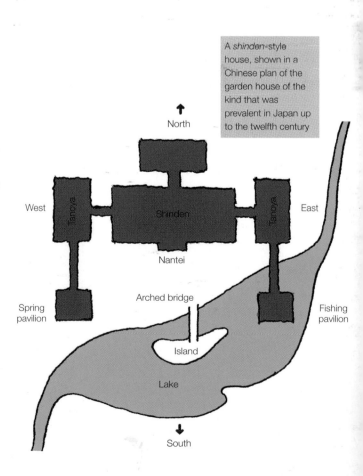

A *shinden*-style house, shown in a Chinese plan of the garden house of the kind that was prevalent in Japan up to the twelfth century

North

West

Tanoya

Shinden

Tanoya

East

Nantei

Arched bridge

Spring pavilion

Fishing pavilion

Island

Lake

South

Pages 42–3:

In the garden of this Kyoto restaurant clipped bushes balance the tension created by the steep slope of the trunk and branches of the pine tree, the shadow of which follows the *nosuji* of the site.

Left:

In this section of the garden in southern Corsica, which was designed by Erik Borja, the sea was hidden behind many evergreen oaks. In a reversal of the metaphorical approach but in a move that took account of the wider environment of the site, a few of the trees were removed, making it possible to incorporate the rocky outcrops into the garden as crane island.

Right:

Another view of the same seascape, this time seen through a narrower frame.

The Shakkei or Borrowed Landscape

It is important at this point to emphasize the idea of framing, which is an essential aspect of Japanese gardens. At the beginning of the thirteenth century the symmetrical, imposing *shinden* style was abandoned in favour of an asymmetrical, irregular approach to architecture, which permitted the development of a form of house and garden that was more in keeping with Japanese sensibility and taste. Most of the main rooms in these new houses opened on to gardens, with sliding doors revealing either part or all of the outdoor space. Depending on the sightlines, there would be a view of a small area of the garden or the whole area, the geometric limitations of space emphasizing its art-like nature and making it comparable with an engraving or a painting. We shall find this use of framing again in the garden and beyond, in the technique of the *shakkei* or borrowed landscape. Within the confines of a temple the *karesansui* (dry garden)

was often bounded by walls or clipped hedges, against which arrangements of stone stood out. These boundaries not only isolated the garden from the outside, but also focused the view on the foreground, giving it its own scale and reinforcing the effect by dividing up the space. Beyond the garden, however, when the surroundings provided an interesting view of a wooded mountain or hill, this background would be 'captured' and used to counterbalance the garden. 'Capturing' a striking landscape requires some special care when a garden is being planned. The layout of the garden must incorporate the background into the main composition without making it too noticeable, thus preventing the outside garden from dominating the composition, which would destroy the harmony of the whole.

The borrowed landscape often takes another form. In large gardens, where the space is not limited by walls, openings on to the landscape can be positioned to provide the visitor with unexpected pictures. The trimmed plants act as a

Left:

A view of the landscape to the west of the garden in southern Corsica that was designed by Erik Borja. There is a purification stone in the foreground, while the mountains that may be seen across the bay contribute to the overall composition of the garden.

frame, gently linking the different scales and incorporating them into a whole. Here, too, a proper balance is necessary, and the landscape should not be borrowed to the detriment of the garden. For example, if the garden is in a dominant position on the side of a hill, the plants should frame the most interesting sections without ever revealing the entire panorama, which would result in the garden being overpowered and its character destroyed.

In this chapter I have outlined the main rules that govern the design of a garden. We must now deal with the use of shapes and the main features that are used in the composition of Zen gardens and that, once understood, could be used in other garden schemes, whether or not they have a Japanese theme.

Right:

A very old juniper, clipped into cloud topiary, stands out against the sparkling surface of the gulf inlet to the east of the house in the garden in southern Corsica, which was designed by Erik Borja.

STONE FEATURES

'You should position the stones while observing the features of the garden and the orientation of the pool. Express the fusui, which may evoke a natural landscape, and keep the original shape of the stones in order to do this.'

The Sakuteiki

Striking-looking rocks are given their own identity within the Shinto tradition, which reveres them as the homes of spirits, and cults grew up around their original locations. As Japan opened up to Sino-Korean civilization and adopted its architecture, the practice arose of placing stones in the garden, which, in addition to their decorative function, had the purpose, according to Chinese cosmogony, of protecting the house from evil spirits. Unlike the Chinese, the Japanese avoided choosing stones for their gardens that were too ostentatious or odd or that had strange outlines because the Shinto culture associated the spirits of ancestors and deities with perfect manifestations of nature. In order to avoid the risk of negative elements jeopardizing the harmony of the garden, only perfect stones were selected, a choice that also suited the aesthetic sense of the Japanese, which tends towards simplicity and authenticity.

In the end, it was this aesthetic aspect that became dominant in the Zen period. In rejecting superstitions, Zen gardeners used stones in the garden as essentially artistic features. At its zenith, the Zen garden was limited to nothing but an arrangement of rocks, in which the individual stones, freed from any religious, symbolic or metaphorical associations, were used for what they were as much as for what they represented. The stone garden was reduced to a purely abstract entity, representing only itself, and in so doing it became universal. What strikes us today in these stone compositions is their fluid art and the formal, subjective beauty arising from it. In addition to the particular meanings attributed to each one is a sculptural art, which we admire and which draws its strength from the apparent simplicity of the rough stones, transformed by the gardener into a work of art.

In all their manifestations, stones appear to be an essential component of the Zen garden, and the structure or backbone of the garden is created through the arrangement of the main pieces. The wide variety of materials and shapes available and their strong powers of suggestion offer scope for the use of stones as metaphors and symbols. They may represent the three major themes of the Zen garden – the mountain, lake and islands – and other features, such as the waterfalls, water courses and mythical figures, like the turtle and the crane in metaphorical form, but these representations remain deliberately vague, because it is up to

Right:

A stone boat stands out against the backdrop of vegetation in the garden of Daisen-in, Daitoku-ji, Kyoto.

Left:

In the garden of Ryogen-in, Daitoku-ji, Kyoto, a mountain stone symbolizes Mount Horai, the Mountain of the Blessed in Buddhist mythology.

Crane island seen from the southwest corner of the garden of Ryogen-in, Daitoku-ji, Kyoto. The highly maintained raking is characteristic of this modern garden.

the onlookers in the Zen garden to approach each arrangement of stones and choose the viewing angle according to their own mood. It is a personal and individual decision each time. Various approaches are possible, therefore, and this makes interpretation difficult. An erect rock, for example, may just as easily arouse thoughts of a mountain, an island or an animal as it might suggest a waterfall, thoughts taking wing or even the Buddha.

The 'Soul' of Stones

Because the concept of beauty occurs only rarely in Japan, when we discuss stones and rocks we refer instead to their 'soul' – that is, what they 'say' to us and what images they evoke. Nevertheless, the choices made in terms of the images they suggest determine whether the garden succeeds aesthetically. Not all rocks have sufficient character to be representational or even to feed the imagination. A pebble, for example, no matter how beautiful it may be, cannot suggest a mountain or be used as an erect stone, since its surfaces have been eroded by the action of water and are too smooth to evoke the unevenness of a mountainside. It should instead be used to represent a river or the side of a valley.

Large stones should be used to emphasize focal points such as the pools, islands or mountains. In order not to destroy the subjective view the garden offers, it is better not to use stones that are so large that they destroy the balance of the garden and jeopardize the representation of the universe as a microcosm. The rocks must be of the same kind as those that originally existed on the site to make the arrangement both realistic and harmonious. If there are no stones on the site on which the garden is to be planted, it will be necessary to find a source of stones of the type that would originally have been in the garden in order to avoid introducing inharmonious elements into the arrangement.

The entrance to the garden of Myoshin-ji in Taizo-in, Kyoto, was designed by the architect Nakane Kinsaku in the 1960s. The garden itself dates from 1500.

The garden of Chishaku-in, Kyoto, dates from the twelfth century and represents Mount Rozan in China, a place of inspiration for monks and poets. The 'folding screen' stone to the right of the waterfall exposes its *hare* (meaning sun, heaven and yang in Japanese), while the opposite side, *ke* (earth, moon and ying in Japanese), remains in shade.

These remarks apply only, of course, to groups of large stones. Smaller stones, particularly those in streams or that appear just below the surface of the water should be in keeping with the water feature, and their eroded appearance or coloration can be used to highlight the roughness of the rocks around them.

There are some rules about the use of stones, the most important of which is that they must not be used in a different way from their natural position. A stone that is found lying on its side, for example, must not be placed vertically and vice versa. The original placement must be respected, and each stone must be re-positioned in the garden as it was originally found. This is crucial if their original 'nature' is to be preserved. A stone found in shady undergrowth and covered with moss or lichen will quickly lose its beauty and character if it is exposed to full sun.

Basalt columns in Erik Borja's garden in the Drôme, which were excavated from volcanic vents in the Massif Central, change from grey to bluish-black according to the humidity in the air. They emerge from clumps of tightly clipped lonicera.

Collecting the Stones

There are no suppliers of rocks in France as there are in Japan, and it is necessary, therefore, to make a note of the positions of suitable rocks when you are out walking and to obtain permission before removing them, particularly if you want to move large numbers of stones. Under no circumstances should quarried stones be used in a Zen garden because the process of extracting them from the ground reduces them to the level of debris, with no sheen or soul. Some areas abound in stones of every kind, and it is easy to obtain suitable examples, particularly for use in small gardens.

Finding the main stones and choosing them requires a great deal of time, and heavy equipment is sometimes needed to transport them to, and arrange them in, your garden.

In addition, you should have ready to hand a stock of stones of different shapes from which you can select the most interesting to achieve the best possible arrangement. After much practice you will, as you walk around the countryside, be able to identify the exact stone that is missing from part of the garden. Over time, you will begin to acquire a mental compendium of shapes that will enable you to pick out the stone you are looking for from among a chaotic mass of fallen rocks. Many of the stones I collected at random while I was laying out my own garden have eventually found their appropriate place, even the insignificant ones, whose very ordinariness contributes to the cohesion of the whole.

Examples of ways in which groups of three stones can be arranged. Generally, stones are positioned in groups of three, five or seven.

'Do not arrange stones in too abrupt or sophisticated a manner but rather tentatively.'

The Sakuteiki

Using Stones

There are two types of surface in the Zen garden – the soil covered with gravel, moss or herbs and the pool, which is used to counterbalance the soil – and they are generally brought to life or emphasized by the use of rocks.

Arrangements of stones, which were influenced by the monochrome paintings from the Sung period, express a poetic atmosphere, rather than a real landscape. Because the garden belongs more to the imaginary than the real world, it is not a question of reproducing but of translating the sensations and emotions that certain sites arouse.

The stones must, therefore, be positioned to face the ways they did in nature and not be disorientated. They should never be treated as if they are simply objects that have been brought in.

As you lay out the main stones, you create the mountain, pool and islands, the focal points of the organization of space in the garden. Garden construction in Japan has always started by identifying where these features are to be located and defining their surface area and volume. Other features – waterfalls, bridges, lanterns and purification stones – are included only to accentuate or emphasize part of the site.

We shall consider the pool in the next chapter, but here we will deal with the mountains and islands, which can be represented in many ways.

Mountains

Representing the landscape when they are used alone, mountains also provide a backdrop for other elements, such as plants, and are the source of streams or waterfalls gushing from their slopes. Their outlines reinforce the *nosuji* of the site, defining the outline of the pool and the shape of the garden's perimeter.

Because the mountains act as a backdrop to the garden, their scale must be in keeping with that of the garden itself so that they appear as natural as possible. You will find it helpful to look at some actual examples of the kind of effect for which you are striving in order to understand the principles involved. In nature mountains have wide bases because of the effects of erosion. If the mountains in a garden are to convey the power and height of the real thing, their bases must be anchored in solid, stable ground. Under no circumstances should they simply rest on the soil's

Right:

To build up the side of this artificial slope in the garden in southern Corsica designed by Erik Borja, existing outcrops of rock have been filled in with stones of the same colour and texture, creating the impression of a massive structure.

surface. The bases must be buried so that only the interesting part of the stone juts out above ground. Clumps of appropriately sized plants may sometimes replace banks of earth or be used to add bulk in larger gardens.

The mountain must be seen as a whole, and the group of rocks representing it must underline its structure, expressing its natural power and dramatic height. To achieve this effect, the structure and volume of the stones used must be carefully and subtly grouped so that the composition enhances the overall lines and emphasizes their attributes. It is the interaction of the individual stones that creates the image and brings out the balance and rhythm of the garden.

It is rare that an individual stone will be large enough to represent the mountain by itself. Usually, tall, upright rocks are accompanied by smaller stones, which should enhance the main stone, emphasizing its character and reinforcing the sense of movement. The accompanying stones should be arranged around the central stone to create the effect of a mass of fallen rocks, which conveys not only an impression of instability but also a sense of the interaction of surfaces and angles. The subsidiary stones, which are often laid around the base, give an impression of bulk and should appear to have the same source as those that will be arranged on the slope. These additional stones, decreasing in number towards the summit, will lead the eye up the mountain and to the *oku* stone. Unobtrusive, set back somewhat, rather isolated and almost hidden, the *oku* stone introduces a third motif into the composition, completing it and representing its culmination.

In gardens where the terrain makes it impossible to create a mountain, stones that are sufficiently large and that will produce an interesting structure may be used to represent it, on their own or with other stones. Groups of three, five or seven stones, in a variety of shapes and positions, can be arranged in a meandering line, running in the direction of the

The side of the 'mountain' in the garden of Sanzen-in in Ohara, to the north of Kyoto, is completely man-made. It is made up of large stones and clipped bushes, which seem to hurtle down the slope towards the pool in artfully arranged confusion.

An imposing stone 'mountain' at the entrance to the garden of Tenjuan in Nanzen-ji, Kyoto, welcomes the visitor. The moss and gravel areas intertwine in a somewhat ill-defined manner, as in a pen and ink sketch.

nosuji, to create the impression of mountains as seen in the distance. The associated planting must not destroy their scale.

This style of composition is also suitable for small gardens, but the modest nature of the scale and composition demands that the stones be of the highest quality. Their shape and appearance must be sufficiently evocative to give the illusion of an archipelago seen from the sky and a sense of space.

In such a garden the hills may be represented by low, moss-covered mounds of earth. Their outline

and profile must follow the *nosuji* of the site, enhance the stone mountains and look like a rocky base that has been formed by erosion. To give greater depth and rhythm in a limited space, these mounds can be of various heights, and the shadows cast will accentuate the different levels.

In this interpretation of the 'mountain' in the garden of Nanzen-ji, Kyoto, the group of erect stones is balanced and counterbalanced by the stone lying in the foreground.

Right:

The garden of Tofuku-ji, Kyoto, was designed by Mirei Shigemori in 1938–9. In the right-hand portion of the southern garden the gently rolling mounds, which are covered only in moss, are in keeping with the very positive composition on the left of the garden (see page 71).

Below:

In the garden of Nanzen-ji, Kyoto, as in the garden of the temple itself, stones and plants fill in the gaps in the representation of the mountain.

Islands

In the *shinden*-style gardens of the Heian period the island is associated with the mountain. It symbolizes Mount Horai, home of the gods and the Buddhist representation of the universe. It was assimilated by the Japanese into their archipelago, where, they believed, the topography corresponded with the mythical view of the Islands of the Blessed. The island was originally assumed to be moving, drifting across the ocean with the currents, until a sea spirit stabilized it by supporting it on the back of a turtle, the symbol of longevity, Paradoxically, although it is part of the world of water, the turtle also represents earthly stability.

The island, which came to be called turtle island, was introduced symbolically into gardens of the Heian period, and since the twelfth century it has been linked with crane island. The crane is the symbol of the sun and immortality and represents the migration of the soul. In Buddhist mythology the crane accompanies the soul of the dead to paradise.

The two islands, opposites yet complementary, contribute to the cosmic balance, become inseparable and are often represented in the gardens of the *shoin* period by arrangements of stones. Their outlines differ. Turtle island has a simpler, more compact shape that recalls the overall outline of the animal whose name it bears. In contrast, crane island is longer and is composed of several stones, some of which are upright in order to capture the spirit of the air and the flight of the soul.

Crane island in the garden of Rokuon-ji at Kinkaku-ji, Kyoto. Numerous islands, planted with nothing but pine trees, are dotted over the pool. The scale of the trees is kept in proportion to the surface area of the water,

The more compact turtle
island in the garden of
Rokuon-ji, Kinkaku-ji, Kyoto,
is topped by pines, while the
stone on the left suggests the
head of the mythical animal.

This interpretation of the island in the garden of Tofuku-ji, Kyoto, is characteristic of modern designs, which often use large stones to portray islands.

Left and above:

Crane island in the southern garden in the Drôme, which was
designed by Erik Borja in 1997. The vegetation in this garden,
especially the pine tree, which will eventually cover the head of the
mythical bird (seen in detail above), has not yet achieved its final
shape and size.

Crane island

Turtle island

Above:

Opposites in symbolic meaning, turtle island (representing stability) and crane island (representing the migration of the soul) are frequently linked in gardens.

Left:

The animated artistic appearance of the very old juniper, only a few branches of which are still alive, dominates turtle island in the garden of Konchi-in, Nanzen-ji, which is attributed to Kobori Enshu (1579–1647).

Although the arrangement of the rocks used to create crane island and turtle island may resemble the outlines of the mythical animals, like any stone compositions in the Zen garden they must also provide foundations for the vegetation that will eventually grow on their surfaces.

Below:

In the garden in southern Corsica, designed by Erik Borja, the original stones have been enhanced by clearing away the vegetation that concealed them.

Above:

Sanzonseki or 'stones of the three saints' stand in the garden of Daisen-in in Daitoku-ji, Kyoto. The three stones, which differ in height, symbolize the Buddhist triad.

The Sanzonseki

A stone composition originating in Buddhist mythology, the *sanzonseki*, or 'stones of the three saints', is a group of three erect stones of slightly differing sizes, the tallest of which may be about 1.5 metres (5 feet) high. Placed on a northeast–southwest diagonal – a path adopted by evil spirits – its function was to trap the spirits and force them to the ground and, with the help of the stones facing towards the west and south, to remove them, thereby protecting both the garden and the house.

These three vertical rocks were often used to suggest a waterfall, and sometimes different layers of smaller stones would be arranged at the base to form a dry fall.

The group is one of the most positive and dynamic of the aesthetic features found in the Zen garden.

Right:

The rich texture of these modestly sized stones in the garden of Daisen-in in Daitoku-ji, Kyoto, gives them remarkable powers of suggestion.

A detail of the geometric paving stones of the *shiki-ishi* type in the garden of Tenjuan in Nanzen-ji, Kyoto.

Paths

In contributing to the overall image of the garden, Japanese paving stones, paths and walkways around the house offer a variety of ways, both visual and structural, in which stone can simultaneously play aesthetic and utilitarian roles, including having such mundane uses as allowing people in the garden to avoid walking on mosses or muddy ground.

At the entrances to temples and houses ornamental paving stones were cut and arranged to mark out the walkways and guide visitors to the main entrance. Crossing small reception gardens, the paving linked the public and private areas. In a Zen garden the use of paving stones is limited to outside the boundary of the building and garden, but they may be used as purely artistic elements in gravel or mossy areas to emphasize an important arrangement of stones. This type of geometric, structured, ornamental paving is called *shiki-ishi*.

In the garden of Tenjuan in Nanzen-ji, Kyoto, the paving stones follow the *nosuji* of the site and are an essential element in the garden's overall design.

In meditation gardens black, glazed paving tiles, generally edged with a gutter that takes water from the roof, run alongside the passageway and provide a walkway at garden level, which is shaded by the roof canopy. The water course, made up of cut granite edging and black gravel, marks the boundary beyond which the dry or wet garden extends. These uses of stone on the ground are always linked to the accompanying structures and contribute with them to a geometrical organization of the overall space.

In other types of garden – tea gardens or water gardens, for example – where it is possible to stroll, paths are indicated by paving tiles, the style and form of which vary according to the space or atmosphere the designer wishes to create. The *tobi-ishi* form, made of natural, uncut stones in a meandering path, may here be added to the *shiki-ishi* form.

Smoothly cut stones that are easy to move are generally used for these paths. Anchored on a bed of coarse gravel, grit or moss, or embedded in the hard-packed surface from which they emerge, they are positioned to suggest a pathway laid on water and to make an irregular pattern on the surface of the soil. Both the choice of materials and the arrangement of the stones used in both styles can vary widely.

These stone paths mark out the space and help visitors, whether they are walking or standing still, to find their bearings within the overall garden.

Their importance varies according to their position. In tea gardens, which have a rustic feeling and include untamed undergrowth, natural stones are arranged at random in an irregular pattern, as if they have been left as nature intended. The distance between them must allow easy access but appear to have occurred naturally. Their surfaces and shapes must be asymmetric, drawing the eye to the ground around them.

In water gardens, on the other hand, if their size permits, the stones become more important, both as aids to direction and as aesthetic features in their own right. The surfaces of carefully cut and shaped stones, combined with natural stones, make an ever-changing canvas, emphasizing the rhythm of the garden, drawing attention to particular sites and encouraging the visitor gradually to discovery the garden. The careful positioning of paving stones enhances unattractive or too narrow sections of the garden or draws attention to major elements, such as the main entrance to the house.

This use of paving for paths has been found in most Western gardens from very early times.

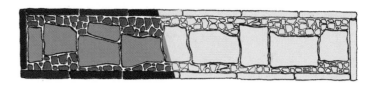

Japanese paving stones of the *shiki-ishi* type

A combination of *shiki-ishi* and *tobi-ishi* stones

Anchoring the paving stones in the soil

Roman mosaics of marble, the paviors in the gardens of the Alhambra and of the Italian Renaissance and as seen in more recent European adaptations of the style have always been associated with a desire to model the design of the garden on that of the house.

In Japan, on the other hand, the garden is seen as another world, and one that is entirely unconnected with the living area. It is nature, not architecture, that dominates. Once the threshold of the house is passed, one enters a world of dreams and of the imagination, and all the elements that make up the garden must contribute to this impression of unreality.

Japanese paving stones of the *tobi-ishi* type

Broad *shiki-ishi* paving at the entrance to a temple in Kyoto.

The interaction of style and material between the *shiki-ishi* path and the gutter in Kyoto.

Page 83:

Shiki-ishi and *tobi-ishi* paving stones are linked in Erik Borja's garden in the Drôme. The paving has both an aesthetic and functional role, both guiding visitors as they discover the garden and preventing them from walking in mud or on mosses.

Below:

The threshold to the private garden designed by Erik Borja in the Drôme. The visitor's stone and the host's stone face each other on either side of a symbolic boundary.

Right:

Tobi-ishi-style stones in Kyoto. This irregular paving is often used in tea gardens.

Right:

Another example of a *tobi-ishi* path, this time from Erik Borja's garden in the Drôme. The stones of the paths are inserted into a bed of cobbles, which suggest a river.

Left:

Paving stones in the *tobi-ishi* style lead to the threshold of a pavilion in Kyoto.

Bridges

Bridges sometimes provide a link between islands or across narrow streams. Because it crosses purifying water, a bridge appears to be a passage-way between two worlds, a transitional area evoking the spiritual elevation that makes the island, which symbolizes paradise, accessible. The *soriba-shi* style, which evolved from Chinese tradition and which, with its semicircular curve, is unsuitable for people to use, is reserved for the use of the spirits, the *kami*. The bridge's reflection in the water suggests the moon's disc.

In all other styles, the bridge, whether it is made from natural rocks or constructed in wood or cut stone, both serves to symbolize the purifying crossover and also helps to guide the steps or direct the eye. As with paths, the use of

*'The location of the bridge must not coincide
with the axis of the shinden.'*

The Sakuteiki

Above:

In the small garden of Daisen-in in Daitoku-ji, Kyoto, the bridge is represented by a shallow stone only about 10 centimetres (4 inches) deep.

Left:

The bridge in this larger area is on a human scale.

Right:

As in the garden of Chishaku-in, Kyoto, bridges are often used as symbolic, artistic elements, emphasizing by their horizontal nature the dynamic of the banks of stones and plants that make up the garden.

bridges is always linked to the search for a deviation from the main line or a change in orientation, slowing down progress and guiding the visitor towards this or that detail or point of view. The bridge is the equivalent of the changes in tone that are characteristic of Japanese music and poetry. As a structural element, the bridge – together with lanterns and the *torii* (the gateway to a Shinto shrine or holy place) – implies that people are present and, through its shape, contributes to the style and appearance of the garden.

Whatever its form or style, the lantern often symbolizes the presence of humans in the garden, whereas the tree represents the sky and stone represents the earth. The lantern is itself made up of five elements, which assume a three-fold symbolism. The two upper sections represent the sky, the two lower sections the earth, and the central section represents humans, caught between these two worlds.

Lanterns

Stone lanterns, which were originally votive objects at the entrance to temples or in cemeteries for honouring the souls of ancestors, underwent a change of function and were introduced into gardens in the Zen period as aesthetic elements. They are also used as a representational indication of the presence of humans in the garden.

Many different styles are used, ranging from imposing, ornate lanterns to modest collections of stones that merely represent a lantern. When they are combined with the *chozubachi* purification stones, they may also, depending on their size and location in the garden, be elements in a composition. Most of the lanterns are not actually there to light the garden; they are, instead, primarily artificial features used to mark out a space, balance a composition or attract the eye to a particular perspective or detail. The variety of shapes, materials and heights makes it possible to find a lantern that is appropriate for all manner of schemes and designs, and whether they are used as central or subsidiary objects in the garden, they bring a human dimension into the composition.

Opposite:

The lantern in the garden of Koto-in in Daitoku-ji is used to give emphasis to the view. It contributes to the balance of the elements in the composition – tall maples, the bamboo forest and moss-covered ground.

WATER IN THE GARDEN

Water, the source of life and a symbol of purity, is always present in some form in Japanese gardens. A gravel surface completely enclosed by a dry garden may, metaphorically, evoke a vast ocean or a lake surrounded by mountains. As a mirror of the sky and receptacle of the light of the stars, water gives the garden character and depth, while its course and position govern the overall design. The calm surface of a pool and the lively water of streams, springs, waterfalls and fountains express the disparate rhythms, music and emotions that accompany travellers who discover something new each day.

The Pool

The pool, whose smooth surface makes it the focal point of a garden, enhances the undulating hills and slopes and provides an additional dimension. In the Zen garden the size and outline of the pool will reflect the scale and form of the whole, and the remainder of the garden can be laid out in reference to them.

According to the rules drawn up in *The Sakuteiki*, water should enter the garden from the north-northeast and, passing around the house to the south, leave in the southwest. Because the lie of the land will not always permit this, steps can be taken to remedy the situation artificially by making a few appropriate adjustments, or it may be possible to break the rules and simply allow the geography of the site to dictate the route the water takes, because the overriding aim is to express poetically a harmonious relationship with the wider environment. Nevertheless, it is always important to locate correctly the points at which water arrives in and leaves the garden and to make sure that as it crosses the garden the water follows the site's *nosuji*.

So that the surface of the water remains clear, the size of the pool will be determined by the flow of the spring, stream or waterfall that is feeding it. If it is to remain unclouded, the water must be continually replaced. When the pool is being designed, therefore, it is important to take into account the general direction in which it flows. If the speed and volume at which the water flows are carefully thought through, they will carry vegetable and organic matter away from the pool, and oxygenating plants will help to purify the water. If the water flows too slowly in relation to the surface area of the pool or if it is in direct sunlight or if the water is not deep enough, algae will form, upsetting the ecosystem and quickly taking over. If, however, the pool is fed by a stream flowing at the correct speed, it will be straight-forward matter to install a pool.

Opposite:

In the Botanical Garden, Kyoto, the pool occupies a dominant, central position, and all the plants are reflected in it. The light from the sky, captured on the surface of the water, helps to light up and bring life to the lower portion of the view.

In the garden of Sanzen-in in Ohara, north of Kyoto, the pool is more intimate and more sombre. The autumn colours of the leaves bring the surface of the water to life.

Right:

The water in the garden of
Kaku-ji, Kyoto, is almost
invisible, but the presence of
exuberant aquatic plants
indicates the existence of a
pool that is, in fact, largely
open to the sky. The mass of
plants surrounding it is
enhanced by the smooth
surface of the water.

Left:

In the Botanical Garden,
Kyoto, the surface of the
water creates a mirror effect
and provides indirect light,
which lights up and magnifies
the pattern and colour of the
maple branches.

Once the pool has been dug out, the base and sides are lined with a layer of clay 20 centimetres (8 inches) thick. When this is tamped down and covered with gravel, it will provide a good seal. If the pool is constructed on well-drained land it is sensible to use a flexible liner laid over a prepared, well-trodden-down layer of sand. The pond liner will follow the contours of the pool and, if a special protective under-liner is used, it will not be damaged by stones in the base of the pool. The bottom and edges of the liner can be masked by gravel and stones, making them appear natural. Aquatic plants can be grown in perforated plastic containers, which will allow them to be moved when the pool is cleaned. Reinforced concrete can be used to construct small pools, but all the surfaces must be covered with rocks, and the area must be sufficiently large that the surface of the water is not too restricted once the stones have been arranged.

Not everyone, of course, can have a natural stream in their garden. If the water supply comes from the public water mains, a well or a bore hole, it must be oxygenated and residues of chlorine or phosphates removed from it by exposing it to the sun. Before it flows into the pool, the course of a stream in which stones will be laid can be constructed so that they will encourage oxygenation by breaking up the current. In dry areas the aim should be to restore to the water table the volume of water that is taken out to fill the pool and keep the water recirculating.

Stones can be used in a number of ways to provide the general outlines of the pool, including rocky peninsulas, steep banks, strips of land and deep bays. The few plain lines – gravel beach, landing stage, fields and so on – accentuate the character of the rocky areas. The choice of stones – their shape, size and texture – must be as in keeping as possible with the environment of the area dealt with. The way the pool sides, peninsulas or islands are created must suggest the violence of the sea. Rocks torn from the cliffs, promontories and reefs will be enhanced by the positioning around their base of half-submerged stones, the strata of which will recall the foaming waves. The

Stepping-stones, cut from granite rocks, allow visitors to walk across this magnificent large *shinden*-style pool at a Heian shrine in Kyoto.

beach will be created from gravel whose size and shape are appropriate for the scale of the pool, and the entire area will have an artistic appearance, just as if it had been created by the strokes of a pen on the surface of paper.

Waterfalls

It was, paradoxically, during the Zen period that the waterfall became a major feature of the garden. Water is the source of life, and Zen monks celebrated it in all its forms, particularly in the *karesansui* (dry garden), where it was suggested by arrangements of nothing but stone. From this period onward the real or symbolic waterfall became the focal point of the entire garden, and *The Sakuteiki* gives a great deal of advice on its construction. The pattern of the water and the style of the waterfall depend on the stones used and the way they are arranged. Through its lively, dynamic nature, cascading water is one of the most important components of the garden and, depending on its shape and height, is open to a wide variety of interpretations.

Whatever style is adopted, the waterfall is always constructed from the base upwards. The way the rocks are arranged guides the eye from the surface of the pool to the top of the waterfall and the real or implied mountain from which it gushes. There are several rules determining its form. To begin with, the bed of rocks emerging from the surface of the pool must appear to be sufficiently stable and solid to be a convincing and realistic base for the wall and the stones that are erected on either side.

If the waterfall is higher than 1.5 metres (5 feet), the *mukai-ochi* (twin falls), *kata-ochi* (a fall emerging from a single point) or *kasane-ochi* (tiered falls) are preferable. In the *kata-ochi* and *kasane-ochi* styles stones should be positioned to create obstacles that will change the shape of the waterfall and the sound it produces. At the top the stones should be arranged so that the water appears to gush from a dark, concealed place in the side of the mountain, like a spring. The overflow stone guiding the water will determine the shape of the waterfall, while the water's arrival in the pool, whether direct or indirect, is usually partly masked by a stone emerging at its base. Two stones at the sides frame the waterfall; they are *ke*, the yin side, which is in the shade and is vertical, and *hare*, the yang side, which is in the sun and is horizontal. They are interchangeable, depending on the position of the waterfall in relation to the house. If the axis from the *shinden* (house) is situated towards the right, *hare*, jutting out slightly, will get the sun, while *ke* will be in the shade. But if it is on the left of the *shinden*, the left side will become *hare*.

The guidelines established for building waterfalls are also valid for dry falls. Although the use of metaphor allows great freedom of composition, it is difficult to evoke the leaping course of the water and the roar of the waterfall because the stones are motionless. The power

Mukai-ochi (twin falls)

Nuno-ochi ('fabric' fall)

Kata-ochi (a waterfall with water emerging from one side)

of suggestion must be rigorously applied in the dry fall or the balance of the whole will be destroyed.

Here we find one of the major principles underlying the approach of gardeners of the Zen period: not to attempt to imitate nature through too realistic a representation but to transcend its manifestations and, through artifice, reveal its essence in a union of the whole. In dry falls, gravel arranged on the slope of a dry stream will be sufficient to evoke the tumultuous cascade of water, and an expanse of gravel will represent the calm surface of a pool or ocean waves. The

way raked gravel areas in dry gardens are designed helps to recall the movement of waves. Their regular pattern emphasizes the surface of the rocks and refines the composition into an abstract form. When we contemplate some Zen gardens it is no longer a landscape we see but a sculpture that exists on its own terms, even if it is created in materials borrowed from nature.

Because waterfalls have become one of the focal points of the garden, we may be surprised to find that they are almost always constructed in dark, unobtrusive places. Often we are able to locate them only by their sound. Their presence may be

Ito-ochi (ribbon fall)

A combination of two types of waterfall, the *sowa-ochi* style (spaghetti fall) and the *kasane-ochi* (tiered fall)

Kasane-ochi (tiered fall)

as subjective as it is real. Experienced rather than actually seen, the waterfall contributes to the overall garden, and, because it is set back, it does not dominate the scene. Too spectacular a waterfall would destroy the harmony and balance of the garden as a whole.

Springs and Streams

The same principles appliy to springs and streams, whose point of entry into the pool must follow these guidelines. Sound plays an important part here, and the noise made by the water must be discernible and harmonious, neither too intrusive nor too subtle, but in keeping with the nature of the waterfall, spring or stream.

Creating different sounds by rearranging stones in a stream is a fascinating exercise. Interrupting the flow of water creates a murmuring, musical sound. According to this typically Japanese approach, the suggestion that water is present – arising from its sound – allows us to be content with, for example, a slow flow rate and a modest volume of water entering the pool in order to evoke a mysterious, secret spring.

Below left:

Mukai-ochi (twin falls) in the southern garden in the Drôme designed by Erik Borja.

Below right:

A *kata-ochi* style of waterfall at the Heian shrine, Kyoto.

Opposite:

The bottom of the dry fall in the garden in southern Corsica, which was designed by Erik Borja. The stream of water is suggested by green serpentine stones, which are laid as a path between the granite rocks leading to the calm surface of the gravel pool.

Purification Stones

The *chozubachi* (literally, 'hand basin') purification stones are another way in which water is brought into the garden. The stones were originally laid out in front of Shinto shrines so that pilgrims could wash and purify themselves before joining in the worship. Like lanterns, these religious objects became features in the composition of gardens from the thirteenth century.

The *hachimae* purification stones are placed in the garden along the edges of the paths at a height at which you can wash your hands without having to crouch down. They can be found in tea gardens in the low form, *tsukubai*, which simply means to crouch down, or in the form *shizenseki* (literally 'kimono sleeves'), which is a natural stone with an indentation in its upper surface. Fed by a fountain made of bamboo, the water overflows from the basin and covers the rock face, reviving the colour and surface texture of the rough stone.

Purification stones are sometimes little more than receptacles for rain water. A small bowl placed at the edge of a pathway means that the

Below:

In this dry garden, the stones laid in the bed of the stream evoke the tumultuous course of the water.

plants around can quench their thirst and the stones can be moistened so that the onlooker can contemplate the colours that are revealed in the water. Even in the tiniest gardens, where there is nothing more than a lantern, a few rocks and plants, the *chozubachi* will introduce the refreshing, vital presence of water.

Left:

A purification stone of the *shizenseki* type in the garden of Rokuon-ji, Kinkaku-ji.

Left:

A purification stone of the *hachimae* type in the garden of Tenjuan, Nanzen-ji.

Right:

This *hachimae*–type purification stone, in the garden of Sanzen-in in Ohara, north of Kyoto, is positioned beside a path and raised from the ground so that visitors can wash their hands without crouching down or even having to enter the garden.

Fish

In the Heian period gardens and their pools were filled with animals – mainly birds, such as cranes, herons and ducks – and also with fish and turtles, but their use died out somewhat in Zen gardens and with the development of dry gardens. Only fish and turtles were kept in water gardens, and their presence brings the waterscape to life in a pleasing fashion as well as contributing to the ecological balance. Koi carp, whose wide variety of colouring gives rise to spectacular collections, are well-known fish, which quickly grow accustomed to your presence and will come towards you, looking for little treats. Birds and wildlife of all kinds will soon find their own ways to bring life to these spaces, but you must be careful with herons or cormorants, which can empty a pool of fish very quickly. Construct deep areas in your pool and provide rocky shelters where the fish can be protected from predators.

THE PLANTS

'According to Buddhist doctrine, one day a millionaire wanted to dedicate a marvellous temple to Buddha, but was unable to find the right trees to build it. In those days, a priest of princely origin thought that dedicating a temple decorated with treasures to Buddha was one thing, but dedicating trees was quite another, also worthy of Buddha. So he dedicated trees and made a garden.'

The Sakuteiki

Plants are present everywhere in the daily life and aesthetic philosophy of Japan of both yesterday and today. Despite the modernization of their lifestyle, the Japanese remain firmly attached to the use of plants as a raw material for creating objects and for building.

As points of reference for aesthetic values in all kinds of applications – packaging, signs, kimonos, roof tiles, crockery or cast iron gutters – images of plants of all types dominate everyday life. They indicate to visitors to the country the strong relationship between the people and their environment. Even the language is dominated by them, as the names of colours, pastries and dishes are derived from the plant world. The exuberance of plant life in Japan, which results from the favourable climate, is obviously a determining factor in the importance given to flora in everyday life. Paradoxically, in gardens the model seems to have developed from what is rarely found in the Japanese landscape except in places such as mountain peaks and rocky sea promontories, where the difficult climatic conditions purge nature of what grows abundantly in more sheltered sites.

Highlighting what is 'rare' is a constant theme of any artistic undertaking. Sometimes the simple act of separating a camellia flower from its bush reveals its individual, unique beauty, when it is not evident as part of a whole. Plants are used in this way in the Zen garden, where maximum effect can be achieved with great economy of method. This gives greater importance to the subject by refining its form, by removing distractions or by clarifying its shape or texture through pruning a tree or weeding an island of moss and helping it transcend its original nature.

Autumn colours appear on the maples that grow along the banks of the Katsura River, to the west of Kyoto.

Zen Trees

In Shinto and Buddhist tradition trees have the power to capture beneficial heavenly flows. It would seem that planting trees in gardens not only attracts the gods but also protects the house and its occupants from negative forces. Although

Left:

In autumn the leaf colour of maples, such as those growing in the Botanical Garden, Kyoto, is highly prized by the Japanese, who grow large number of maples in their gardens because they admire the special light that they produce.

Below:

When the cherry trees have lost their foliage, the dry bamboo structure supporting the branches can be seen. These trees are in the garden of Tenryu-ji, Kyoto.

hundred-year-old trees are revered within Shinto shrines, the trees that grow in gardens are not the object of any particular veneration. Unlike the old trees, which grow freely in their original form, the trees of Zen gardens are pruned, shaped and structured with a great deal of care in order to restrict their growth and to give them an artistic, ornamental dimension that will be in keeping with the style and scale of the garden. The Zen gardener adopts a minimalist approach and experiments with a restricted tonal quality of plants. *Cleyera ochnacea*, known in Japan as *sakaki*, remains the sacred tree par excellence, but it is not as often found in the Zen garden as pine, maple or cherry trees.

During the early part of the Heian period (794–1185) the plum tree, which had been imported from China, emerged as the most prized flowering tree for gardens. It remained in favour until the middle of the ninth century, when the Japanese mountain cherry (*Prunus jamasakura*; syn. *P. serrulata* var. *spontanea*), the symbolic tree of spring sites, supplanted it. The same is true of the maple, which grows in densely populated areas in northeast Japan but was not used in the southwest until later when it colonized gardens and escaped into the surrounding landscape. The cherry tree and maple, which change the colours of forests and gardens in spring and autumn, helped to produce a new aesthetic vocabulary. They codified seasonal themes, establishing relationships between plants, seasons and elements of Japanese thought and literature. The Buddhist tradition of marking the seasons was somewhat blurred in the Zen period, as the timeless character of the gardens did not involve the idea of seasonal change. Conifers, particularly pines and trees and shrubs with evergreen leaves, are preferred simply because they give the gardens an unchanging, timeless aspect, like a painting or drawing frozen for all time in a fully defined and controlled form.

Cherry Trees

Many types of cherry tree are used to decorate gardens, but those with downward-hanging branches are preferred. Cherry trees are placed only rarely within the true Zen garden, but they cover the surrounding countryside, which acts as a backdrop to the garden. They are grown for their blossom, and pruning became a factor in the Zen period chiefly to encourage the flowers.

Elaborate props of dry bamboo are used to support the branches, forming tunnels under which people can stroll. Every year in April and May the blossoming of the cherry trees is an event in Japan, and crowds travel to admire them. The light filtering through these tunnels of pink flowers, whose petals are strewn across the ground, gives an unreal, magical aspect to these walks. The enthusiasm for them is such that after dark the underside of the branches is illuminated by braziers, and great numbers of people come to picnic under the boughs and celebrate the blossoming of the cherry trees.

Maples

The full-moon maple (*Acer japonicum*) is also left to attain its full size and usually grows freely. So that the autumn colours are perfect, however, the foliage is thinned out by pruning. The crown can be lightened so that the sun filtering through it pigments its leaves. Towards the end of November crowds throng into the gardens to admire the colours of the maples as they do with the cherry blossom in the spring.

The tree's graceful shape, achieved through the artificial lengthening of its branches, has an airy lightness that is different from the compact, stocky shape of the cherry trees. The maple is sometimes grown as a bush, when it is pruned into a semi-bonsai, and in this form it can be incorporated into the Zen garden. Generally, however, the maple, like cherry trees, cryptomerias and other large trees, is usually planted as a decorative backdrop, on the neighbouring hills or in the small gardens in front of the Zen space.

Above:

In April the appearance of blossom on the cherry trees is an eagerly awaited event, celebrated by the entire population, who crowd into the public gardens. The Buddhist tradition, which marks the passage of the seasons, reveres the cherry and maple as trees that symbolize the enduring cycle of nature.

Pages 112–13:

In the garden of Koto-in in Daitoku-ji, the artistic interaction between the evergreen foliage of the bamboo and the ephemeral colouring of the maples marks the passing seasons.

Right:

Autumn colours are intensified by their reflection in the water in the garden of Ryoan-ji, Kyoto.

Pines

Oddly, the pine, which can be seen in gardens everywhere, particularly in Zen gardens, is neither as revered nor as celebrated as the cherry tree and maple. The evergreen foliage does not mark the passing seasons, and, as far as I know, it is not the subject of any of those Japanese rites that emphasize the seasonal cycles. But it is precisely this timelessness that makes it the Zen gardener's favourite tree. It is used in abundance in every garden and often seems to be the main subject of a composition, with a single tree sometimes evoking an entire forest.

In Japanese mythology the pine is associated with the crane, the sacred bird and symbol of immortality. In its upright form, the pine adorns crane island, but it also often crowns turtle island, and here pruning is used to give the round, compact shape of a shell. Podocarps lend themselves particularly well to pruning, which in Japan involves techniques that are, to my way of thinking, a little too drastic. In most cases, however, pruning is still selective and aims to reinforce the artistic effect of the trunk and branches. This work, which consists of removing the small branches and pruning the hard wood, can be carried out throughout the year if the diameter of the branches is not too important. Having selected the large, interesting branches, their design can also be tidied up and refined by removing the twigs on the main branches that deviate from the desired line and shape.

Because the Scots pine (*Pinus sylvestris*) lends itself to every style of pruning, its position in the garden and its use in the overall composition determine its style. On some species of pine the bark is stripped away from the trunk to reveal its orange colour, which is in keeping with the garden's autumnal hues. At the start of spring, when buds begin to appear but before they flower, two-thirds of them must be removed at the top by pinching them out by hand. This time-consuming but vital work preserves the horizontal regularity of the branch's foliage by removing vertical shoots. At the same time the previous year's needles are thinned out on the young branches, leaving only a small corolla at the base of the pinched-out bud.

This stripping of the shape is carried out so rigorously in Japan that after pruning, the trees have the air of small boys coming out of the barber's shop, their hair cut short behind their ears! With this technique, however, the new shoots quickly take on an artistic, slender aspect, which resembles the idealized pattern created by the tree.

Many other conifers lend themselves to this degree of reshaping. In Japan cryptomerias, thujas, maidenhair trees (*Gingko biloba*) and in the south of France junipers, varieties of *Chamaecyparis*, *Cupressus arizonicus*, cedars and almost all the large-crowned conifers are suitable for this treatment. The size to which they are pruned should, of course, be consistent with their natural growth, and we should not go against the laws of nature but allow ourselves to be guided by the characteristics of the tree and avoid over-pruning, which would turn the trees into caricatures.

In Japan pines are regularly cut and pruned. The process prevents the over-abundant growth of foliage and encourage branches to form interesting patterns.

Pruning to Reveal

The methods used to shape trees and shrubs may seem cruel and unnatural to Western gardeners, but Zen gardens originate in artifice and in this context we are concerned with the re-creation of nature, not with its conservation. Nevertheless, nature can be transcended only by someone who has a profound knowledge of plants and their peculiarities, which pruning can enhance without changing their fundamental character. It is therefore vital to observe trees and shrubs closely as they grow naturally in order to be able to choose the appropriate pruning size for each one.

Linear Pruning

Within the confines of the Zen garden it is preferable to use species that are slow growing and slow to mature. Even though regular pruning limits their growth, some vigorous species may grow too large within a few years and destroy the scale of the composition. It is better to plant such trees at the edge of the Zen garden, where their size can act as a backdrop, stand in for a missing hill or

indicate an area of distant landscape. Because of their size and function, the technique that is used for shaping is closer to lopping than to the pruning used for subjects in the foreground, and because it is more natural, the technique makes the integration of the garden into the surrounding environment easier.

Two trees of the same species are placed in the foreground of the garden space and in the area used as a backdrop to it. The tortured outlines of pines, standing as isolated, tormented subjects and kept small, may, by their contorted form, suggest a seascape beaten by the winds and the spray. This is in keeping with their size in the scale of the Zen garden. When they are planted beyond the limits of the garden and incorporated into the landscape they need to be pruned accordingly. This will leave only a few top branches and will strip the trunks, so exploiting their height and enhancing the clump of plants from which their elegant outline will emerge. By highlighting these plants, they will draw the eye and create a visual link between metaphor and reality.

This so-called linear pruning, which consists of promoting the artistic qualities of a tree by revealing the shape of the trunk and branches, can also be applied to large shrubs, including camellias, *Lagerstroemia* spp., photinias and privets, and also arbutus, mastic (*Pistacia lentiscus*), evergreen oaks, box (*Buxus* spp.) and hollies. The structure of all these shrubs lends itself to this type of pruning.

Compact Pruning

Bushes, on the other hand, are trimmed into a compact shape, called *karikomi*. They can be handled as isolated subjects, *kokarikomi* (small

In the garden of Sanzen-in in Ohara, north of Kyoto, the eye is drawn to the ground, where clipped bushes form a dense, structured landscape, while the trees shading it in the background have kept their actual scale

clipped bushes), which are reminiscent of traditional Japanese tea plantations, where the bushes were always pruned into regular spheres. Alternatively, they can form a mass, *okarikomi* (large clipped bushes), as a monumental shape representing a mountain or a mass of rocks and used as a backdrop to the main subject of the composition.

Small-leaved bushes with a dense habit are the preferred kind, usually azaleas, such as *Rhododendron* 'Satsuki', but box (*Buxus* spp.) and the evergreen *Eurya japonica* can also be used. If the land and climate do not lend themselves to these species, *Lonicera nitida*, heather, myrtle and dwarf *Pittosporum* spp. can replace them. By planting them as close together as possible and pruning them several times a year, it is possible to achieve large shapes. Access has to be provided so that the gardener can get to the row of plants to prune them without crushing them.

It is vital to use well-sharpened pruning shears. Young shoots are pruned to about 1–2 centimetres (½–1 inch) so that the wood is not stripped, and it is, therefore, necessary to prune at regular intervals. The effect must be natural, evoking the effect of shoots cut off by sea spray or spring frosts. The soft, regular shape must look as if it has been sculpted by the winds, and, depending on their size, the shapes of the bushes will suggest verdant hills, steep mountains, a stormy sea or islands in the ocean.

The *kokarikomi* approach is different. The bushes are clipped separately, generally into balls, irregular in size and texture, and they rest on a support, embankment or hill, which they partly cover. These clipped bushes form a more varied and complex landscape, and they act as a counterbalance and support to rocky outcroppings. They may even mask weaker sections, completing and balancing the stone compositions. They can also be used to accentuate the edge of the pool or stream and to frame the waterfalls. These bushes,

almost all of which are evergreens, may be of different species, and it is acceptable to experiment with several varieties of foliage and colouring. Nevertheless, it is important not to overdo the diversity if you want to construct a coherent, calm landscape. The overall harmony would suffer from contrasts that are too emphatic and too sudden. Through the play of light and shade, the plantings provide relief and depth to the backdrop of the pools or surfaces of raked gravel.

Above:

Pruning the pines at the Heian shrine, Kyoto.

Below left:

Loniceras trimmed into small bushes (*kokarikomi*) and heather trimmed into large bushes (*okarikomi*) in Erik Borja's garden in the Drôme.

Below right:

Linear pruning has been applied to this dwarf mountain pine (*Pinus mugo*) and Portuguese laurel (*Prunus lusitanica*) in Erik Borja's garden in the Drôme.

Maintaining the Shape

If the shape of a Zen garden is to be successful, the gardener must keep it at its best throughout the year. To achieve this the plants must be regularly and carefully pruned. Pruning times vary according to the plants, the speed of growth of their foliage and the flowering cycles of the tree or the bush.

The artistic aspect of Zen gardens also comes from intensive weeding of all surfaces, whether they are covered with moss or gravel or are just trodden earth. In Japan the gardeners pay scrupulous attention to maintenance through-out the year. In spring and summer weeds are removed by cutting their roots with a knife so that the moss is not damaged. The undergrowth, paths and gravel areas that represent the sea are swept every day, and any leaves that have fallen from the trees are cleared away unless it has been decided to leave the red leaves of the maples or the flowers of the cherry trees strewn over particular surfaces to achieve a pleasing effect, when the coloured carpets are renewed each day by new flowers or freshly fallen leaves, whose beauty has not been spoilt by the rain or by visitors standing on them.

Everything in the garden must be just as if it were drawn with a pen stroke on paper. It must have the same clarity as a drawing, and it should appear to be an entity and as close as possible in its detail to an idyllic view of nature – in a word, heavenly.

Working with Nature

Although there are wide differences in temp-erature between northern and southern Japan, the entire archipelago has a temperate, coastal climate that, with the regular monsoon, gives it the advantage of a having soil with a signifi-cantly high moisture content. The water table and the subsoil must be saturated if the plants are to prosper without the need for artificial

Right and below:

Okarikomi pruning is used for rosemary and loniceras in Erik Borja's garden in the Drôme.

Below:

A large number of tools is needed to maintain and prune the garden. As with a surgeon's equipment, they must be thoroughly cleaned and carefully sharpened after use.

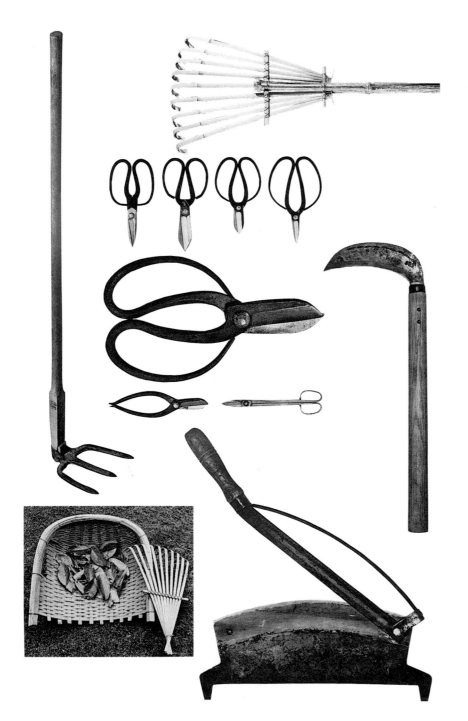

watering in summer. The seasons are, nevertheless, differentiated by the growth of vegetation. The fields, for example, turn yellow in summer and keep their golden colour until the weather turns cold, and stubble-burning, which is carried out each year at the end of the winter, is enough to maintain them. Some mosses in those parts of the garden that are exposed to the sun turn a brownish colour in dry weather, but they regain their colours as soon as the rains return, and this does not appear to affect their growth.

In this respect the Japanese are faithful to the Buddhist tradition, for they appreciate these climatic variations and do not try to fight them. In addition, they know that drought and cold are necessary for a garden's well-being. If plants are to do well, they must meet their nutritional needs themselves. A lack of water forces them to develop deep roots, which will make them more robust and, even if they sometimes suffer, they will be resilient and will eventually achieve a balance. During the first year, however, the Japanese spray new plantings a few times to help them get established, particularly bare-rooted plants, which are better planted in autumn so that they can survive the winter and spring with a good root system already established.

Pages 122–3:

Tidying up the garden of Tenryu-ji, Kyoto, in the autumn. In Japan gardening and garden maintenance are seen as aspects of asceticism and as ways of practising religion.

As here, in Erik Borja's garden in the Drôme, plants from your own area can be used to make a Zen garden. Pruning is what gives the garden its character.

It would be futile to aim to plant the same varieties and species in our countries as are grown in Japan, simply because the climates are so different. By carefully observing the surrounding environment, the climatic conditions, the quality of the water, the degree of moisture in the air and the nature of the land, plants and trees can be selected that will best suit the chosen site. Even if it is possible to alter the character of the land by adding new topsoil or fertilizer, only those plants that thrive in your area should be chosen for long-term development. In the Drôme, for example, the continental climate and the hard water do not lend themselves to growing azaleas. Heathers are used instead and, after pruning to control their shape, they flower profusely and extensively. The Mediterranean climate is suitable for bushy plants such as myrtle, mastic (*Pistacia lentiscus*), cistus or rosemary, which have a similar dense appearance. Even if the flowers are not as beautiful as those of azaleas, the results are as satisfactory. The Scots pine (*Pinus sylvestris*), on the other hand, has small needles and adapts to any climate and to any land, and it can be used almost anywhere in the northern hemisphere. Plants are given their character by pruning, and you should, therefore, always choose plants that grow best in your garden. You should approach the problems of plants' adapting to different growing conditions in a relaxed frame of mind: carry out your own experiments and draw lessons from them. The plants you choose will make an original display of your garden, even if the garden itself borrows the essence of its vocabulary from Japanese gardens.

My Garden Studio

In my gardens in the Drôme in the south of France all the force lines around my house run from west to east. The road leading up to the house, the rows of vines surrounding it and the slope on which it is laid out converge on the river in the east. Situated on the edge of the plateau, surrounded by vineyards to the west and north, the building makes an L-shape, with its walls to the east and the south. It was in these two directions, following the site's *nosuji*, that after restoring the house, I gradually completed a series of five gardens, which today constitute a whole. This space is still my laboratory, my experimental field where, throughout the years of turning failures into successes, I have tried to create a garden where my plans could come to fruition. By describing my venture in a step-by-step way I hope to be able to help you understand the meaning of the rules for making a garden and the way in which the artificial features of the Zen garden work in Japanese-style designs.

The five gardens are the meditation garden, the tea garden, the Mediterranean garden, the river garden and the southern garden, and their relationship to my house can be seen in the plans on pages 127 and 146.

The Meditation Garden

The garden occupies a small triangle bordered with vines to the north and the edge of the slope that descends to the orchards in the south. From the main wall a vast landscape can be taken in of the wooded banks of the river and the orchards below, the plain and the mountains of Vercors and the Alps beyond. But the foreground was not satisfactory. This triangular field was devoid of trees, and the existing bushes were only brambles and scrub. Swept by the northern wind – the

Left:

The entrance to Erik Borja's gardens. Rising above bushes clipped in the *karikomi* style (here, santolina and lonicera are linked), an Arizona cypress (*Cupressus arizonica* var. *arizonica*), trimmed into a cloud shape, welcomes visitors. A flowering apricot tree (*Prunus mume*) unfolds its slender branches under the shelter of an umbrella pine (*Sciadopitys verticillata*).

Mistral – and burned by the sun, this stony ground produced only poor, arid vegetation. I had to change it all so that a garden could blossom. At first my ambition was limited to making a small garden. Sheltered by the corner formed by the north wing and the main wall of my house, I intended that the garden would occupy the foreground, establishing a visual link with the landscape and capturing it in some way.

There were several reasons governing my choice of the Zen theme for this first section. Apart from the keen interest I had in this type of design, the confined space, my modest means and the little time I was able to devote to this work encouraged me to produce a reasonably sized garden. The style, however, would provide a strong, structured foreground, a subjective view of the real landscape, incorporating the house and the site. Because the north wing protected only a small part of the garden and because the limited space meant that we could not build a mountain, I contented myself

with raising the ground slightly along the vineyard and planting a mixed hedge there of trees and shrubs to act as a wind-break to the Mistral. Extremely dense and made up of evergreen plants trimmed into an undulating, irregular mass, the hedge represented the missing mountain, diverting the harmful effects flowing from the north towards the river in the east. It also helped to frame the meditation garden, which I planned to lay out in front of the main wall.

The rural architecture of the Drôme is far removed from the Japanese model. Nevertheless, I did not alter the character of my house and did nothing more than lay *shiki-ishi*-style paving for walking and standing on. This replaced the covered, raised passage from which the garden is traditionally gazed upon in Japan.

Beyond this space extends the *nantei*, a neutral area marking the border between the real and imaginary worlds. Only gardeners cross this symbolic line; onlookers may enter it only by

Right:

A detail of part of the gardens immediately surrounding the house in the Drôme.

1 Entrance to the reception garden
2 Reception garden
3 Entrance to the private garden
4 Tea garden
5 Meditation garden
6 Mediterranean garden
7 Purification stone
8 Lantern
9 Spring
10 Crane island
11 Turtle island

A drawing of the all the gardens in the Drôme viewed from the south.

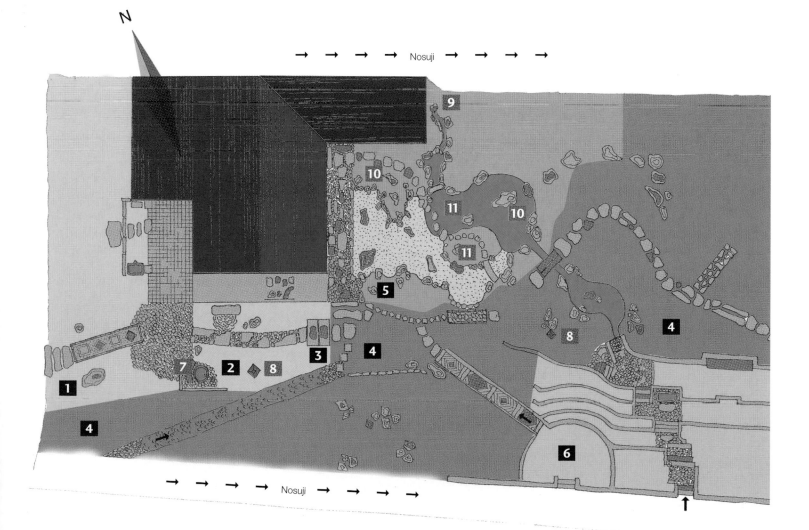

N

→ → → → Nosuji → → → →

→ → → → Nosuji → → → →

looking and by gazing on it as a work of art, as a painting. I gave it the form of a pool. Covered with white gravel, this metaphysical space evokes an expanse of water on which rocky outcrops suggest the reefs and banks of a seascape. It spreads out towards the southeast over about 10 metres (33 feet) at its longest, its width being almost equal to that of the eastern wall of the house on to which it backs. On its right are banks of clipped shrubs, which not only enclose the space but also draw the attention and direct the eye towards the far end of the garden, where a gap opens on to the landscape below. With their backs to the south and in the shade of two albizias, in summer these shrubs help to establish a microclimate and maintain the humidity needed for mosses and plants to grow. To complete the composition and rebalance the light in the garden, I excavated the water course on its left at the base of the north hedge. Fed by a diverted spring and carried to the northeast corner of the house, and extending the expanse of gravel on the left around which it skirts, it then branches off towards the south and the large pools. Its reflective surface brings life and light to this part of the garden, drawing the eye and directing it towards the arrangement of stones, which relies on the foliage in the tea garden beyond, which is trimmed into the shape of hills.

Left:

The paving that borders the meditation garden in front of the east wall of the house suggests a ford across a river.

Right:

A stone boat floats on an imaginary pool.

Pages 130–31:

The meditation garden at sunrise, opening at the far end on to the tea garden. On the left, crane island, which is surmounted by a Scots pine, meets turtle island on the right. Turtle island is covered with moss, from which emerges a *Cotoneaster horizontalis.*

A detail of the small pool,
which extends the gravel area,
forming the point at which
metaphor and reality meet.

The 'head' of crane island faces the southern section of the meditation garden.

The entrance to the tea garden at the beginning of the slope.

The Tea Garden

The tea garden lies to the east and south, bordering the meditation garden.

In Japan, unlike the meditation garden, the tea garden provides the visitor with a path leading to the tea ceremony pavilion. The tea garden originally led from the house to the pavilion where the tea ceremony took place. The origin of this rite dates back to the fifteenth century, a period when the country was in a state of continuous civil war. At the time the religious élite felt the need to impose a ceremonial etiquette by which, during a truce, opponents in power struggles had to make their minds a blank. They were forced to rid themselves of their passions and share with their enemies tea that was prepared for or by him. This practice, which became so highly ritualized that it became an art form, imposed civility and extreme politeness on those involved and compelled them to get to know each other better and, possibly, to get on together. The wild, natural garden was originally laid out as a journey of initiation, designed to calm the visitor's bellicose tendencies by its beauty and poetry and to encourage both visitor and host to have a clearer, more dispassionate view of each other and, ultimately, to make peace with each other.

I have used this style of garden in the areas that are available around the house and the meditation garden, to which it acts as a backdrop. Designed to be discovered gradually, it is made up of several separate sections, linked by paved paths. It begins at the point where the road reaches the garden in the west and extends as far as the eastern point of the slope, from where it dominates the southern garden.

The water enters the pool. Because it is situated on the left of the meditation garden's gravel area, it is not visible from the *nantei*, and its presence is revealed only through its murmur.

The first section, along the south wall, is made up of two small reception gardens. A purification stone at the entrance, sheltered by tall trees and a dry bamboo hedge, allows visitors to refresh themselves, while a bench invites them to rest a while. A Japanese lantern emphasizes the presence of humans in the garden. Only the murmur of the water falling into the basin disturbs the silence. This contemplative pause helps put visitors into the frame of mind that will enable them to breathe in the atmosphere and soak up the poetry of the place before approaching the host, who waits in a private garden.

Access is generally through a portico, but this is absent here because of the architecture of the nearby house. Two flat stones lie facing each on the ground – the visitor's stone and the host's stone – and these are framed by shrubs, clipped into clouds. The garden then unfolds over the side of the slope, skirts around the meditation garden and occupies the remainder of the triangular until it ends in the east.

Flowering trees with deciduous or evergreen leaves provide shade. Bushes, mosses, low-growing

The arrangement of three erect stones, or *sanzonseki*, in the tea garden, represents the Buddha and two Bodhisattva.

A detail of the paving that crosses the reception garden and leads to the tea garden. The two types of stones, *tobi-ishi* and *shiki-ishi*, meet here.

plants and rocks are arranged along the sides of the path and provide variety and a range of atmospheres. Borrowed landscapes are used here and there, revealing gardens and orchards to the south. Tall trees have been planted below on the other side of the slope in the first section and at the far end of the garden in the east for coolness and moisture retention. They are sufficiently far away that they do not destroy the deliberately small scale of the meditation garden. I have used the garden element of the traditional tea garden only, adapting its vocabulary and form and building the pavilion close to the southern pools in order to avoid a proximity to the house that would be anachronistic.

These first two gardens were sketched out, then revised and improved over several years before the balance was achieved. The continual changes in growing plants must be supervised and observed for a few seasons yet, but the rocks, paving and water course are now finally in place.

Opposite:

A juniper (*Juniperus* spp.) and an Arizona cypress (*Cupressus arizonica* var. *arizonica*) frame the entrance to the garden and replace the *torii*, the traditional portico marking the threshold of the private area in Japan.

Below:

Japanese paving stones in the tea garden guide the visitor towards the southern gardens below.

Basalt columns and clipped
banks of *Lonicera nitida* on
the southern slope of the tea
garden are used to represent
the male and female symbols
of the yang and yin.

Kept to a smaller scale by pruning, the plants give the illusion of a vast landscape which, in reality, does not exceed about 10 square metres (108 square feet).

Opposite:

The closely pruned juniper, clipped into cloud shapes, contrasts with the freely flowering daylilies (*Hemerocallis* cvs.) at the southeast corner of the house.

Pages 144–5:

The snow-covered meditation garden. The snow accentuates the graphic aspect of the garden and disguises its imperfections.

I am a self-taught man, and I took an intuitive rather than a scientific approach as I started my work. Over the years the experience I gained through practice and from studying gardens in Japan and the rules governing the way in which they were created made me better able to overcome the problems that arise in making this type of garden. Because I was unconstrained by dogma, I was able to progress more freely into a design form that was not familiar to me. I understood that the significance of ritual does not lie in the meaning of the deed, but in the act that it involves.

I produced a preliminary version of these two gardens between 1973 and 1978, but because I was again living again in Paris in this period I was able to devote only a few weeks each year to them. Each time I returned to Paris I did so reluctantly, abandoning my gardens to the weeds, and during each of my absences, I felt frustrated and missed the gardens more and more. A visit to Japan in 1977 had confirmed my feeling that I had found a new approach, a richer field of research and discovery than I expected. I had learned from my art studies that while it is not vital to understand, it is essential to feel and that a work can best be understood by approaching it with sympathy. It confirmed my view that the subject, details and meaning are of secondary importance to the substance. The artist's style and technique transcend the subject matter to reveal an inner truth, mediated by the artist's humanity, and this universal emotion touches and overwhelms us. Whatever its external form, the work as a whole is, above all, the most accurate self-portrait of its designer there could be. It was, therefore, without too many scruples or regrets that I gave priority to the garden and abandoned my studio, giving myself up completely to this adventure.

Left:

An opening in the pyracantha hedge links the tea garden to the Mediterranean area.

Opposite:

From the terraces, which are built with reclaimed materials, it is possible to look over the pools and orchards to the south.

The Mediterranean Garden

By the early the 1980s, when I had put a lot of work into the flat areas around the house, the gardens were able to spread towards the south, near the running water there. The stony, arid character of the slope caused me problems, as did its position between the top gardens and the space below where I planned to lay out a large pool and waterfalls. The area was crossed by the path leading to the river and did not lend itself to a Japanese-style extension of the garden. I decided to put these disadvantages to good use and to establish a Mediterranean area here. You may be surprised at this choice, which is so very different from my earlier work, but cultivating a paradox is not alien to Zen practice. By treating it as a transitional area or link and because it overlooked the entire landscape, it would be possible to contemplate the southern garden I proposed to create from these terraces.

I employed salvaged materials in the garden's construction, using a wide variety of structural items, each bearing the patina of the passage of time. Drawing on memories of my childhood in Algeria and of my daydreams about the archaeological site of Tipasa, I wanted to create the effect of a ruin rebuilt into a garden, a memorial that would connect me to my origins. Largely composed of stone and with an orderly, rational character, it is dotted with aromatic Mediterranean plants, which fill it with their

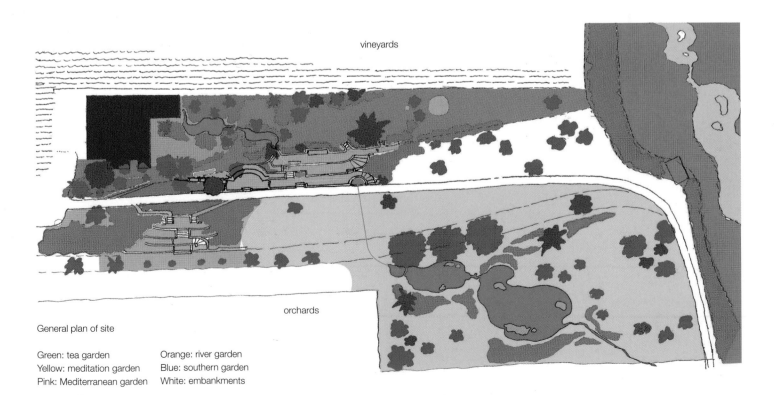

vineyards

orchards

General plan of site

Green: tea garden
Yellow: meditation garden
Pink: Mediterranean garden

Orange: river garden
Blue: southern garden
White: embankments

Water from the tea garden crosses the terraces and flows from fountain to fountain towards the southern pools.

aroma and emphasize its structure by softening it. Water from the Japanese gardens crosses it and flows from fountains into basins on its way south.

The closeness of two gardens of such very different types required some precautions. Clipped hedges and angled paths allow the visitor to stroll from one to the other without ever being able to have an overall view of both. The pathways were treated with especial care so that there would be no unexpected views or surprises. The quality of the stones used for the paving and the low walls plays a major part in this, and the network of paths, guiding the visitor's movements, creates the link and helps to provide the continuity and harmony of the whole. From the terraces, on which there are no tall plants, the view unfolds unimpeded as far as the southern garden, where my plan was to excavate the pools, following the logic of the site and its general orientation.

This sunny space is suitable for aromatic plants, and when the warmer weather arrives, cacti and succulents thrive. Common dogwood (*Cornus* spp.) is used to emphasize the lower part of the terraces in the foreground.

Below:

The variety of materials used for the low walls evokes the archaeological sites I knew in my childhood in Tipasa.

Bottom:

A small bas-relief representing the Minotaur emphasizes the Mediterranean character of this part of the garden.

Right:

Large banks of plants, consisting of trees and clipped hedges, protect the meditation and tea gardens from the heat of the sun.

The River Garden

Three 200-year-old oaks, which I have always regarded as the site's guardian angels, are aligned at regular intervals on the descent to the southeast and to the right of the path. They dominate this area and are located almost at the centre of all the gardens designed since, helping to frame views. Extensive pruning has refined their outlines, and removing the lower branches has opened up a wide view of the land around their bases.

By the side of orchards bordering the land to the south and west, I raised mounds of earth, dividing up the space for future pools. Because I did not have enough earth for this work, I took some soil from the flood meadow that had formed in the east in a loop in the river. When I dug to a certain depth in this area, I noticed that the water circulating in the gravel of the subsoil filled the hole as the soil was removed. The water table I had reached was not far down, but it was still 2–3 metres (6–10 feet) lower than the riverbed. This new scheme deflected me from my original intentions, and I abandoned my design for the

southern garden and instead devoted myself for a decade to improving this space. I had a mechanical digger at the time and was able to excavate some of the earth, following the outline of a dragon-shaped pool and using the nearby river as a reference point. At the time I still did not have an in-depth knowledge of *The Sakuteiki*, but I knew that it recommended making the garden in the belly of the dragon (a symbolic image of the river in China and Japan), with the water rushing through the outer part of the loop.

In the excitement of working on this new layout, I forgot an important point, which, years later, taught me a painful lesson.

I was aware of the danger represented by the closeness of the river, and so I raised its banks by a good 2 metres (more than 6 feet) to protect myself from it. To counterbalance the depth of the pool, in the north I laid out a small pool, lined with stone and some 1.5 metres (5 feet) above ground level. It was fed with water from the meditation garden, and a waterfall linked the two pools. Two islands (crane island and turtle island) emerged from the large pool, and I built a tea house on one bank. Plantations and fields framed it all around. The cool, damp place and the alluvial soil encouraged plant growth, and in few years I was satisfied with the garden.

The strip of land on which the garden was laid out was narrower in the north where the river, coming up to the edge of the embankment, changed course, forming a loop that skirted around the garden before flowing towards the south. The point at which the river approached the embankment, about 10 metres (33 feet) upstream of my land, belonged to a neighbour, who had not raised the narrow banks. And it was here in 1993 that a tremendous flood, made worse by uprooted trees, covered the garden, destroying the greater part of it. It filled the pools with silt, and in the south the force of water carried some of the banks with it. This disaster was both a hard blow and an important lesson.

having wanted to control nature without understanding it sufficiently, and I was deeply ashamed. I could not hold against it the fact that the river was the main agent of this catastrophe. The river had, after all, only followed its nature, which is to burst its banks when it is too full. I had overestimated my ability to act contrary to nature in wanting to lay out a garden without taking sufficient precautions to ensure its durability. At the end of that awful, but cathartic day, I began to think about the southern garden, which I had left in abeyance for all these years and to which I promised myself I would buckle down as quickly as possible.

The Japanese have a special attitude to failure, which they honour in a way they do not regard success. They believe that failure teaches us many things of which we would have been unaware in the excitement of success. The effective management of failure involves asking questions and a thorough, constructive analysis of its cause and effect. In this instance, I learned to have a greater respect for the forces of nature, with which we have to come to terms if we are not to be swept away by them.

Over the years, I have had to deal with the consequences of other errors that, although not as serious as the flood, had some effect on my character, but I must confess that that morning, when I found my garden submerged in a river of mud, was a terrible shock. My first reaction was astonishment, and that was followed by feelings of despondency and shock. But I soon became fascinated by the sight of the power of nature, threatening and untamed, and I stayed out in the rain a long time, looking at the disaster and, eventually, finding a certain beauty in it. This incredible energy made me aware of my vanity in

The southern garden before the pools were built.

Opposite:

The pools in the southern garden seen from the top of the waterfall. They were made in 1997 and the layout of the banks has yet to be improved.

The Southern Garden

This project, which I had put off for a long time, was finally completed in the spring of 1997 in the site originally prepared for it in the early 1980s. I had raised mounds on the originally flat surface and planted trees and shrubs at the edge of the ditch, while I waited for the pools to be laid out. I had had time between these two periods to think about their layout. Situated at the bottom of the embankment, they had to be visible from the first floor of the house as well as from the tea garden and the terraces. The surface of the water, reflecting the sky and drawing the eye downwards, would help to provide a link between the different gardens. Following the logic of the site, the south–east orientation was in keeping with the natural landscape of the river banks. The little stream crossing the garden and tumbling down the embankment would flow quite naturally into it.

I had a huge area here, which was suitable for a wider garden in the *kaiyoshiki-teien* (transformation or conversion) style. Light and shade provide relief and depth in every garden, as they do in this design, where the hillocks separating the pools from the orchard in the south were laid out. Following the east–west lines, their northern face was suitable for mosses, which made a dark backdrop for the surfaces of the pools, the slanting sun lighting them only at the beginning and end of the day. The mass of trees planted in the southwest corner protected them from the full glare of the midday sun. According to established principles, I laid out the water inlet at the foot of the great oak to the north of the garden, using plants to intensify the area of shade from which the spring would gush. The trickle of water that crosses the top gardens was not enough to bring to life the waterfalls I planned, so I increased the flow rate considerably in mid-course by connecting it to the irrigation system I had already installed.

The water, which is carried along underground pipes, falls initially into a small basin, which reduces the pressure of the flow. It then runs over the fall into the first pool, which lies at the feet of the three great oaks. Facing the rising sun, the waterfall receives light at the beginning of the day but then remains in shade until the evening, when the overflow stone is brushed by the oblique rays of the setting sun. This first fall, of the *mukai-ochi* (twin falls) type, is approximately 1.5 metres (5 feet) high and is made of granite rocks. Its size is in proportion to the size of the first pool. The water then flows through a *kasane-ochi* (tiered fall), assuming the form of a small torrent, and, having filled the second pool, leaves again in the south towards the river. On this vast expanse of water, crane island occupies the southern side, standing out against the backdrop of the artificial hill. Turtle island, represented here by a single rock, is laid out in the northern part and lies facing the stream. A shore of gravel and rocky outcrops edge the banks.

same time have their own character and poetry. Although I have mostly followed the precepts contained in *The Sakuteiki*, I have allowed myself to be guided by the objective structure of the place, its *tayori*. If I had not respected this, I would have destroyed the spirit of the place.

I hope that these gardens will, in time and after a great deal more work, express the poetic emotion I have felt in the gardens of Kyoto.

The experience I gained throughout this lengthy process has been of great benefit to me in designing other, often different gardens, which I have since made for garden lovers. This

'Through the tayori we succeed in expressing the fusui.'

apprenticeship in understanding and observing, this union with nature and its forces could be achieved only in practice and by experiencing its difficulties, failures and joys. Studying the gardens of Japan has taught me a lot about nature, but my garden has shown me my inner self. And the real surprise lies here, in the fact that an apparently minor activity such as gardening may at this stage encourage us to be creative and to blossom.

The pools in the southern garden and the banks of the river beyond.

This garden, which has a more light-hearted feel, incorporates fields dotted with copses and trees and relates well to the scale of the surrounding landscape. In the intermediate areas between the various levels of the gardens, the natural vegetation, clipped and restructured, contributes to the coherence of the whole.

It is rare that one site offers so many possibilities for planning gardens that are completely different from each other. I have tried to use the geographical complexity of the area in adapting the types of gardens that, because they are interlinked, form a coherent whole but at the

Right:

A detail of crane island, soon after it was built.

CONCLUSION

Making a Zen garden is an immense undertaking for us novices and requires great determination. But what is, after all, important and fascinating in the process is the practice, the progress and the search for a fruitful dialogue with nature. Learning to look and to feel before trying to understand seems to me the right approach to take with nature. Knowledge comes with time. Modesty, patience and perseverance combined with a capacity for contemplation will be necessary for you to create your own garden. And just as we learn to swim by jumping into water, we can become gardeners only by gardening.

It is not necessary to have a huge site to achieve this type of garden, and I would advise those who are tempted to try to start by working on a small area. Few Japanese people have large gardens. They concentrate on enhancing the smallest available surface area, on treating tiny plots of land poetically through the addition of stones and plants. Working on an unprepossessing place – a small, dark courtyard, for example – and transforming it into a place you want to stop and feel the special, poetic atmosphere is an excellent exercise. The impressive diversity of the gardens that have been developed in Japan over centuries on the basis of this Zen scheme makes me think, like McLuhan, that the message is less important than the medium. Even though all these gardens adhere to the main rules, they are primarily works whose style reveals the inner character of their authors or the people behind them and which seem to be the reflection of a specific personality and sensibility.

A general view of the waterfalls in the southern garden.

Glossary

Chozubachi A basin for washing the hands; a purification basin in natural stone.

Fusui The poetic impression, or spirit, of a place, indicating the dynamic of the movement and the energy released from it.

Hachimae A type of purification stone.

Hare A concept linked to the sun, fine weather, solemn ceremonies, purity and public places. The name is given to one of the stones framing a waterfall; it is positioned where the fall emerges and where it will be touched by the sun, as opposed to the KE stone, which is set back in the shade.

Heian The name given to the period in Japan's history between 794, when the imperial capital was established at Heian (now Kyoto), and 1185.

Hiei Literally, 'the cold mountain'; a mountain to the northeast of Kyoto.

Horai The Japanese name for the Island or Mountain of the Blessed in Buddhist mythology, which is represented in many gardens by a stone or clump of plants.

Ito-ochi A ribbon fall, a type of waterfall.

Kaiyoshiki-teien A so-called 'transformation' or 'conversion' garden, in which the level of the pool may be varied by a system of valves to achieve the effect of high and low tides.

Kami Shinto gods, spirits of ancestors, of former chiefs of clans or villages. Also spirits inhabiting the natural elements – trees, springs, rivers, mountains and stones.

Karesansui *Kare* = dry, *san sui* = water mountain. A dry garden; in the *karesansui* water is represented by either gravel or moss.

Karikomi The simple pruning carried out on bushes planted *en masse*.

Kasane-ochi A tiered waterfall.

Kata-ochi A waterfall, that emerges from a single point.

Ke The house, family and private areas. The name given to one of the stones framing a waterfall, it is placed in the shade, as opposed to the HARE stone, which is in full sun.

Kokarikomi A small clipped ball.

Mukai-ochi A double waterfall; twin falls.

Muso Kokushi Also known as Soseki (1275–1351), the first abbot of the Zen monastery of Tenryu-ji and the designer of the garden's stone compositions.

Nantei *Nan* = south, *tei* = garden; that part of the garden running from the *shinden* (pavilion) to the edge of the water.

Niwa The name given to the gravel surface surrounding a Shinto shrine.

Nosuji Literally, 'nerve, tendon'. The 'flow' according to the rules of cosmology; the line of force in the garden, which underlies the structure.

Nuno-ochi Literally, 'fabric fall'. A type of waterfall in which the falling water may be compared to hanging fabric.

Okarikomi A large, clipped bush.

Oku A background; an intimate interior.

Okuishi The most intimate stone, the most hidden stone, which acts as a counterbalance to the general composition of the garden.

Ryoan-ji The Zen monastery of Kyoto, famous for its garden of fifteen stones, attributed to Soami (late fifteenth to early sixteenth century).

Sakaki *Cleyera ochnacea*, the sacred tree of Japan, the branches of which are used as offerings in Shinto ritual.

Sakuteiki Literally, 'secret book on making gardens'. A treatise on Japanese gardens written at the end of the twelfth century by the monk Yoshitsune Gokyohoko.

Sanzonseki Literally, 'stones of the three saints'. A composition of three erect stones symbolizing the Buddha and two Bodhisattva.

Sayu-ochi A style of waterfall in which the water falls at the front.

Shakkei Literally, 'borrowed landscape'. A technique involving the use of the natural landscape as an ornamental backdrop in the composition of the garden.

Shiki-ishi Geometrically shaped paving stones; paths formed from regular paving slabs, as opposed to the TOBI-ISHI type of paving stones.

Shinden Literally, 'place of sleep'. The name of the central pavilion, open to the south, in houses of the Heian period. The term gave its name to the style of these houses.

Shizenseki A purification bowl dug into the top of a natural stone.

Shoin A study or a desk, but also the room in a house that has the finest view of the garden. The *shoin* style refers to the typically Japanese style of architecture of the twelfth to fourteenth centuries that followed the Chinese-inspired *shinden* style.

Soriba-shi An arched bridge connecting the garden to the main island. The bridge's shape, which suggests the moon's disc and its reflection in the water, makes it unsuitable for walking over. It is reserved for the KAMI (spirits).

Sowa-ochi A style of waterfall in which the fall is broken up into a number of shorter falls.

Tayori The metaphysical, rather than visual, structure of a landscape.

Tenryu-ji A Zen monastery of the Rinzai sect, founded in 1339 (or 1342) by Muso Kokushi.

Tobi-ishi Literally, 'flying stones'. Paving consisting of natural, irregularly shaped stones with a rustic appearance. *See also* SHIKI-ISHI.

Torii A wooden, stone or occasionally bronze gateway, marking the entrance to the purified lands surrounding a Shinto shrine.

Tsukubai A low purification stone, which must be used in a crouching position.

Tsutai-ochi A waterfall with running water.

Yamazakura The Japanese mountain cherry (*Prunus jamasakura*; syn. *P. serrulata* var. *spontanea*), the symbolic tree of spring sites.

The tea garden opens on to the landscape to the east of the house. A mound of gravel evokes Mount Fuji, and a lantern and junipers, clipped into clouds, indicate the end of the garden.

FURTHER READING

Berthier, François, *Le Jardin du Ryôan-ji*, Adam Biro, Paris, 1997

Kazuhiko-Fukuda, *Japanese Stone Gardens*, C.E. Tuttle Co., Rutland, Vermont; Tokyo, Japan, 1970

Motokiyo, Zeami, 'The Secret Tradition of the Nogaku', in *The Sakuteiki, the Secret Book of Japanese Gardens* (trans. by René Sieffert), Albert Skira, Geneva

Rambach, Pierre and Suzanne, *Le Livre secret des jardins japonais* (trans. by Tomoya Masuda), Albert Skira, Geneva, 1973

Teiji-Itoh, *Space and Illusion in Japanese Gardens*, Weatherhill/Tankhosa, New York, Tokyo, Kyoto, 1973

Teiji-Itoh, *Jardin du Japon*, Herscher, Paris, 1990

ACKNOWLEDGEMENTS

I would like to thank all those who have helped me make my dream come true: my companions, Joseph Grimaldi, Christian Coureau and Thomas Herbinet, without whom my gardens in the Drôme would never have become what they are, and to all my friends who, at one time or another, have worked with us and supported us in the venture; Jacky Malagoli and Luc Meunier and their teams in Corsica; and Isabelle Jarry, who gave me much valuable advice.

I would also like to express my gratitude to Françoise Duhamel, Anita Pereire, Anne Simonet, Marie-Françoise Valery, Marielle Hucliez and Louisa Jones, who have helped to make my work known, and to Claire de Virieux, Vincent Motte, Jean-Pierre Godot, George Levêque and Deïdi Von Schaewen, who have taken the wonderful photographs.

My thanks also to Paul Maurer, who has followed my endeavours for a decade and has surpassed them in his own excellent work, and to his wife, Françoise. I would like to thank them for their warm friendship.

Finally, I thank all my clients and friends, who have allowed me to create other gardens and thereby enrich my own life and further my researches.

Photographic Credits

All the photographs in this book were taken by Paul Maurer, except that on page 135, which was taken by Erik Borja. The photograph on page 12 © Photo RMN-J. L'hoir; the photograph on page 13 © Photo RMN-Arnaudet; photographs on pages 4–5 and 6 (top left) all rights reserved.

INDEX

First published in the United Kingdom in 1999 by Ward Lock

© Editions du Chêne-Hachette Livre 1999
English translation © Ward Lock 1999

Original title: *Les Leçons du Jardin Zen*
Illustrated by Paul Maurer
Written by Erik Borja
Translated by Christine Blackmore

Published by Les Editions du Chêne-Hachette Livre 1999

Distributed in the United States of America by Sterling Publishing Co., Inc
387 Park Avenue South, New York, NY 10016-8810

A CIP catalogue record for this book is available from the British Library.

ISBN 0-7063-7855-5

Printed in Italy by Canale, Torino

Ward Lock
Illustrated Division
The Orion Publishing Group
Wellington House
125 Strand
London WC2R 0BB